WAY

The Source

Journey Through the Unexplained

———————

ART BELL
BRAD STEIGER

PAPER CHASE PRESS
New Orleans, Louisiana

The Source

PAPER CHASE PRESS
5721 Magazine Street, Suite 152
New Orleans, Louisiana 70115

Printed in the United States

Dedicated to all those people with minds open enough to explore the outer boundaries of our world and take their own journeys into the unexplained.

A.B. & B.S.

Contents

PREFACE

THE HOW & WHY OF *THE SOURCE*

Why a book about the unexplained? As more and more strangeness enters our world, mainstream authority figures such as the government, the media and others in influential positions are being forced to reconsider their opinions about paranormal origins. It is no longer possible to completely rule out that there may be extraterrestrial life among us: too many people have seen and continue to see too many "weird" things. It is no longer possible to dismiss the significance of the extraordinary powers of the human mind that until recently have lay largely untapped. We can no longer ignore the past while new discoveries are made daily that influence how we view our present and future.

By presenting the various speculative nuances in many areas of the category deemed "paranormal," you, the open-minded reader, who looks for answers to at least a few of these questions, can make up your own mind. By reviewing the information presented in this book, and provoking your mind to reach beyond the conformity that some of the skeptical still attempt to maintain, you can make your own decisions about where you think "the source" of all these happenings lies. Your own insight and experiences will lead you to determine the realities of these phenomena from your own perspective.

The Source came into being because of a natural human desire to know what surrounds our often-routine lives. The book was written to delve deeper, past the surface of our brains often numbed by the rush of this world's daily demands. Too busy to think about the possibilities that lie within, we humans can push our curiosity, a wondrous aspect of our nature that should be nurtured, to some dark corner of our heads. There, then, is where you should start, traveling to that back corner with a good reading light, to invite the perplexities you have swept aside to come out and be articulated and examined.

Why have these two authors teamed for a book of this nature? Art Bell and Brad Steiger each command their own respective spheres of expertise exploring the strange, the unusual, and the unknown. For Art, it started with a radio show called *Area 2000* on KDWN in Las Vegas. Addressing issues that arose as humanity neared the turn of the century, this program gave Art the opportunity to explore two issues he has always been most interested in: the existence of life after death and the possibility of intelligent life in the universe. His own unusual experiences (a precognition experience and UFO sightings) compelled him even more adamantly toward answers to these issues.

Area 2000 was later replaced by the now very popular show, *Dreamland*, originating when Art and Chancellor Broadcasting teamed to do his show *Coast to Coast AM*. *Dreamland* was essentially the same as *Area 2000*, but benefited from being nationally syndicated. As Art says, *Dreamland* is "a program dedicated to an examination of areas of the human experience not easily or neatly put in a box, things seen at the edge of vision, awakening a part of the mind as yet not mapped and yet things every bit as real as the air we breathe but don't see."

Over time, nearly anyone of any note or significance who had expertise, knowledge, or unique experiences in this area of interest, were guests on Art's show. Eventually, Brad Steiger was one of these.

Brad Steiger began his career exploring the strange, the unusual, and the unknown by writing articles on paranormal themes beginning in 1956. For years he wrote a weekly newspaper column, "The Strange World of Brad Steiger," distributed internationally. As a young child, Brad had a mysterious experience that would influence and haunt him all his life. Writing dozens of books on the paranormal and supernatural, selling millions of books worldwide, and receiving much recognition and many awards for his achievements, Brad continued to seek answers to the unexplained. Not only did he make national radio and television appearances, including *ABC Evening News with Peter Jennings* and *This Week with David Brinkley*, but he is featured on a weekly syndicated TV show with his wife Sherry, *Could It Be A Miracle?*

The fact that both Art Bell and Brad Steiger admired each other, and shared common interests and views on the issues discussed on *Dreamland*, made for a good combination. Fans of both men have been delighted with their interviews together so to write a book on a broad range of issues that they have discussed or have written about is logical. The reader and fan get just about everything they ever wanted to know about what Art Bell and Brad Steiger feel about these issues. Compiling first hand accounts of unusual experiences, ideas, theories, and speculation about what it all means, *The Source* will fascinate, provoke, and lend insight into the minds of two of the most influential men in the realm of the strange, the unusual, and the unknown.

In approaching the book, Art's words ring true: "keep your mind open, but not so open that your brain falls out."

Jennifer Osborn
Editor

ONE

JOURNEY THROUGH THE UNEXPLAINED

We invite you to join us on a journey through the unexplained, a vast, largely uncharted, dominion of nearly endless possibilities.

For some, it will, admittedly, be a strange journey, for we are about to enter a world with very few boundaries, a world that appears to lie beyond the reach of the five senses and the imagination of the physical sciences.

It is a strange world where effect often precedes cause, where mind often influences matter, where individuals communicate over great distances without physical aids, and where non-human visitors from other dimensions of reality arrive on a regular basis.

We are certain that you will join us, for we sense that you, like us, do not believe that the Age of Adventure has passed simply because all of the continents have been charted, the oceans have been navigated, Mt. Everest has been scaled, and astronauts have walked on the Moon.

We sense strongly that you agree with us that the greatest adventure for all of humankind still lies in the future. You are among the new breed of adventurers who have the courage to explore matters that often contradict known physical laws and to examine phenomena that don't fit into recognized bodies of knowledge.

At the same time, it is likely that you believe with all your powers of mind that some day all these mysterious occurrences in the world of the unexplained will be found to fit into the total scheme of nature and its laws of harmony and balance.

We have been inspired to journey into the unexplained because each of us has an unquenchable need to know ourselves and the true nature of the life and the universe of which we are individual parts. If such elements of the unexplained as the projection of the spiritual body, the ability to glimpse the future, the facility to convey telepathic impressions, and the capability of communicating with multidimensional beings can be established, then the boundaries of our universe become limitless. It will be seen—as the mystic has forever maintained—that imprisoned within each of us is all that is necessary to unlock all of life's mysteries.

Unfortunately, the conscious minds of the great majority of humankind seem unable to draw upon such knowledge, even though it may have literally been implanted in their brains. On the other hand, as we move inexorably toward the Millennium, it would seem that the numbers of men and women who are becoming aware of such innate truths are steadily growing.

Joining the Company of Impressive Explorers

Those new adventurers who are preparing to begin their quest toward a greater consciousness and a broader definition of what it is to be human may certainly take comfort in reviewing just a few of the highly respectable pioneers who have already taken the journey through the unexplained.

The British statesman William E. Gladstone, who most of his life was an avowed skeptic of paranormal occurrences, finally concluded that such explorations of the psyche constituted "by far the most important" work in the world.

Pierre Curie, who with his wife, Marie, discovered radium, stated shortly before his death that in his opinion paranormal research had more importance than any other.

Sigmund Freud belonged to both the British and the American Society for Psychical Research and said that he wished that he had devoted more time to such study when he was younger.

Carl G. Jung remained actively involved in paranormal research until his death.

Sir Arthur Conan Doyle, creator of Sherlock Holmes, became so involved in exploring the unexplained that he "killed off" his famous fictional detective in order to devote full time to a study of the paranormal.

Nobel Prize winner William Butler Yeats was outspoken in discussing his own paranormal experiences and credited spirit intelligences for inspiring a great number of his poems.

Sir William Crookes, the great physicist and discoverer of the element thallium and the cathode ray tube, conducted an exhaustive study of the paranormal.

The German philosopher Schopenhauer insisted that such phenomena were the most important aspects of human experience and that it was the obligation of every scientist to know more about them.

Sir Alister Hardy, the highly respected marine biologist and Professor Emeritus at Oxford, regarded himself as a "true Darwinian," but granted that the DNA code that determined the physical nature of an individual might not give a complete account of the evolution process. The mental—the nonmaterial—side of life, he admitted, "turns out to be of cardinal importance within the process of Darwinian evolution."

The list goes on and on: Mark Twain, the novelist; Julian Huxley, the biologist; Sir James Jeans, the astronomer; Arnold Toynbee, the historian; Alfred North Whitehead, the philosopher—all concerned themselves with exploring the unexplained.

A Dimension of Peace and Revealing Geometric Designs

Brad had a near-death experience occur at the age of eleven. His skull was fractured in several places and he was nearly scalped by falling under the wheels of a moving farm implement. The way he explains it is:

> I had a sense of identification with the mangled Iowa farm body that I saw lying beneath me on the hay stubble below, but I was growing increasingly aware that that unfortunate lad was not who I really was. The real me now seemed to be an orange-colored ball that seemed intent only on moving steadily toward a brilliant light.

Brad's spiritual essence was seemingly free of time and space and he was able to project his spirit to friends and family at distances away from the tragedy in the hay field.

Then it occurred to me that I was dying. I had an awful moment of panic. I did not want to die...And then the beautiful light was very near to me. I perceived a calming intelligence, a being composed of pure light that projected before me a peculiar, three-dimensional geometric design that somehow instantly permeated my very essence with the knowledge that everything would be all right. The very sight of that geometric design somehow transmitted to me that there was a pattern to the universe and a meaning, a Divine Plan, to life. My panic and my fear left me, and I experienced a blissful euphoria, an incredible sense of Oneness with All That Is. I was ready to die and to become one with the light.

Brad found it impossible to describe for others the geometric design that he had seen as he soared out of his body. Although he can see the geometric pattern in his mind's eye as clearly as he saw it then, it seemed to be ineffable, beyond human description.

For many years, whenever he described his experience to lecture or seminar audiences, however, there would always be a few individuals who had also experienced the near-death scenario. They would affirm that they, too, had been shown some kind of tranquilizing yet revelatory, geometric design, which they also found impossible to describe in mere words.

It wasn't until 1988, when Brad's wife Sherry Hansen Steiger began to conduct healing seminars utilizing computer-derived images of fractal geometry that he had seen designs that very closely approximated what he had been shown during his near-death experience.

Interestingly, each time that Brad relates his experience on *Dreamland* or *Coast to Coast*, he receives a number of letters from certain of Art's listeners who have also seen the geometric designs that bring a peaceful euphoria to those who undergo near-death experiences.

Mutual Longing for Meaningful Spiritual Experience

We hit it off from our very first program together. Neither one of us is dogmatic about his opinions; instead we each strive to be objective in our explorations of the paranormal. We both pride ourselves on being eclectic, remaining open to many diverse points of view.

On his radio programs, Art encourages his listeners to call into his studio and express their opinions and experiences freely, without criticizing or attacking them. He allows his interviewees to relate their subject matter without interruption or commentary, thus permitting his audience to make up their own minds concerning the truth or value of their concepts and ideas.

In his books and articles, Brad recounts the philosophies and the other-worldly encounters of his interview subjects as straightforwardly as possible, thus allowing his readers to make up their own minds about the validity of the accounts and their possible applications in their own lives.

Brad has spent over 40 years investigating haunted houses, exploring UFO landing sites, and undergoing a number of personal mystical experiences that have provided him with subjective proof of his theories. On

Art's side, there has been a certain spiritual longing that has expressed itself in a different way. Millions of minds have been opened to a serious consideration of the paranormal, yet he still searches for a satisfying resolution. As he writes in *The Art of Talk*:

> I have investigated many religions and spiritual ways of thinking, but nothing yet seems to fulfill me spiritually. I believe we have a maker, that there is a God. But I am the sort of person who wants proof...I also want to be assured that there is a life after this one. One big problem I have... is that I am unable to accept things on faith...I am a pragmatist. So far the only faith I have is in what I can see or understand—mostly technical or scientifically supported things.
>
> My popular radio program, *Dreamland,* is an extension of my personal interest in learning about spiritual matters. I am open and still interested in learning all I can about these topics. That's why I will talk about and listen to people who investigate the paranormal, near-death experiences, the possibility of an afterlife, reincarnation, hypnosis, and so on.

A Mystical Adventure in Paris

In June 1998, Ramona, Art's lovely soul mate and wife, whisked him away to Paris, France, to celebrate his fifty-third birthday in the romantic City of Lights.

And then it happened.

When Art and Brad spoke on the July 12, 1998 *Dreamland*, Art shared with his enormous radio audience a dramatic, mystical experience of his own.

He had been lying in bed, drifting into that peaceful twilight area before sleep comes, when he suddenly experienced his consciousness shooting up through the ceiling, through the roof of the hotel, and soaring high above the lights of Paris. Art described it as the most incredible thing and absolutely real:

I've always wanted an out-of-body experience, but I had never had one. I accelerated right up to the night sky, but without the physical sensation of rising rapidly...or even of moving. There are no words to describe adequately this experience. As you said, it's an ineffable experience. You feel elation, ecstasy beyond ecstasy. And it happened to me! I haven't had any experience like it—other than, perhaps, the feeling that I had lying down in the sarcophagus in the King's Chamber in the Great Pyramid.

When I came back to my body, I woke up Ramona, saying, "You're not going to believe what just happened!" And then I just ran out of words. Ramona, of course, is aware of such things and guessed what had happened to me. The experience was so real. And it just happened. No paralysis, no strangeness. It just happened. And I want desperately to do it again!

All Roads Lead to the Same End

We cannot promise each individual reader who joins us on our journey into the unexplained a dramatic out-of-body experience. What we can guarantee is a series of authentic adventures of mind and spirit. We will explore the mysteries of our human origins, the enigma of ancient, lost civilizations, the challenges of encountering extraterrestrial or multidimensional beings, and the grim warnings of contemporary prophets who foresee catastrophic Earth changes in our immediate future. And while we will often discuss the riddles and secrets of outer space, we will never ignore the spiritual treasures to be gained from exploring the inner space within each of us.

Another thing which we have always agreed upon is that each one of these seemingly disparate mysteries of the unexplained—UFOs, angels, demons, aliens, ghosts—may be the manifestations of a single Source. We regard it entirely possible that an intelligence or energy, while universal, can somehow individuate itself in order to convey certain concepts or evolutionary patterns to our species.

So come with us now as we take an exciting journey through the unexplained and attempt to answer many conundrums and riddles that may, in turn, provide us all with a better picture of the Great Mystery.

TWO

THE MYSTERIES OF HUMAN ORIGINS

Whenever Art ponders the many mysteries surrounding our human origins, he imagines the scene in
2001: A Space Odyssey when the man-apes gather
around the monolith that has been planted by extraterrestrial intelligence:

When these primitive ancestors of humankind get
zapped by that monolith, we understand that they
are also given a sudden boost in their intelligence.
I really believe that we have to at least consider
that 'Someone from Elsewhere' interacted with our
species in prehistoric times.

In the great muddle that comprises the Genesis
Mystery, any open-minded person cannot summarily
dismiss the scenario created by Arthur C. Clarke and
Stanley Kubrick for *2001*. An extraterrestrial species
millions of years in advance of our own may have genetically engineered humankind—or at least interacted
with us long enough to teach certain of our distant an-

cestors a number of survival skills and the rudiments of civilization.

Most people probably didn't start theorizing about such far-out concepts as extraterrestrial meddling in human prehistory until the classic film was released in 1968. However, the genius of Menlo Park, Thomas Alva Edison commented circa 1920,

> I cannot believe that life in the first instance originated on this insignificant little ball that we call Earth. The particles which combined to evolve living creatures on this planet of ours probably came from some other body elsewhere in the universe.

And to come from some other "body" in the universe and not simply be "star dust" drifting through the cosmos, "someone" had to transport those building blocks of life to Earth in order to permit living creatures to evolve.

Ancient Peruvian Stones with Astonishing Petroglyphs

If the occasion should ever arise, anyone interested in exploring the possibility of extraterrestrial visitors in human prehistory should not miss an opportunity to arrange an interview with Dr. Javier Cabrera Darquea, a respected medical doctor of Ica, Peru. Dr. Cabrera maintains an astonishing private museum which houses a collection of over 15,000 engraved stones of vast antiquity which appear to depict members of a peculiar humanoid species living contemporaneously with the great dinosaurs.

Dr. Cabrera did not have to mount an archaeological expedition to find these remarkable artifacts. They were discovered on land that his father owns in Sallas. An earthquake provoked a landslide that exposed a large deposit of the extraordinary picture rocks.

Dr. Cabrera's collection of bizarre stones range in size from fist-sized to rather large boulders. And every one of them is covered with eerie petroglyphs—some of which depict five-fingered, pointy-nosed humanoids fighting off giant reptiles with what appear to be Viking-styled battleaxes. Other stones portray such delicate procedures as open-heart surgeries.

Dr. Cabrera is a gracious, friendly man, who greets his visitors impeccably attired in a dark three-piece suit and tie. Although he is understandably somewhat cautious to explain his theories to strangers, once he is made to understand that his concepts of a prehistoric world before our own will not be ridiculed he appears to enjoy sharing his provocative interpretations of the stones.

Speaking with great enthusiasm (be certain to bring an interpreter if you are not fluent in Spanish), Dr. Cabrera states his conclusions that the petroglyphs were fashioned by protohumans who lived in what is now present day Peru over 230 million years ago, during the Mesozoic Era. Furthermore, he believes that those prehistoric humanoids were genetically engineered by extraterrestrials that first visited Earth as long ago as 400 million years.

For those who question such a vast antiquity for the petroglyphs, Dr. Cabrera produces a number of documents from various European geologists and petrologists who declared the stones to be derived from lava flows dating from the Mesozoic Era, highly characteristic of the zone where they were found.

Among the papers he offers to substantiate his claims of accurate dating is a testimonial from Josef F. Blumrich, the NASA scientist who developed the design of the Saturn V and participated in the design of Skylab. In a letter to Dr. Cabrera, Blumrich expressed how deeply impressed he was by the petroglyphs and stated his opinion that the mind-boggling discoveries were authentic.

As he leads his visitors on a tour of his collection, Dr. Cabrera points out various stones that depict otherworldly genetic engineers striving to perfect a progenitor of *Homo sapiens*, using first amphibious creatures, then reptiles, and finally early mammalian life forms.

In their prehistoric genetic laboratories, Dr. Cabrera believes that the lemur, a small arboreal mammal, allied to monkeys, may have provided an important step toward the creation of the prototype of humans. He also proposes that skeletal remains of various stops and starts on the extraterrestrial scientists program of perfecting *Homo sapiens* may be scattered throughout the planet.

Strangely enough, a large number of the petroglyphs depict the protohumans without opposing thumbs. Because even the most primitive apes have opposing thumbs—both in the fossil record and in the modern world—Dr. Cabrera seizes upon this anomaly as further proof that the protohumans created by the extraterrestrial genetic engineers predate the apes.

In his view, the entities without opposing thumbs were designed to become as intellectual as their cosmic creators. They were engineered to be reflective people— scientist, philosophers, artists of the highest order.

Then comes a somewhat uncomfortable element in his presentation. Dr. Cabrera theorizes that those entities depicted on the stones as possessing opposing thumbs were genetically engineered to be the worker bees, those who were assigned to common labor tasks. It is those entities of lower intellectual capabilities with their opposing thumbs who were the ancestors of *Homo sapiens.*

This aspect of Dr. Cabrera's research is similar to that of William Bramley's thesis in *The Gods of Eden,* wherein he states that the human species originated as a slave race that was bred on an isolated planet in another galaxy. Far from our species having broken the bonds of slavery, Bramley speculates that we are still considered property by certain extraterrestrial civilizations. Earth, therefore, is maintained as a kind of prison wherein the human species is controlled by physical hardships, spiritual decay and unending conflicts.

Dr. Cabrera contends that great numbers of the prehistoric humanoids were destroyed by a series of enormous cataclysms shortly after they had accomplished the construction of many great cities and monuments, including the pyramids of Egypt. It was at this time, he conjectures, that the immediate inheritors of the superscientists from the stars, the carefully programmed "reflective humans," recognized the signs of the approaching cataclysmic changes and made preparations to return to their ancestral home planet.

All that remained on Earth were the majority of those beings with lower intellectual capacities, the workers and the laborers with opposing thumbs. The prototypical humans who survived the sinking of continents and the restructuring of the planet became the remote, but direct, ancestors of modern humans.

The doctor further theorizes that an examination of numerous petroglyphs indicates that the alien genetic engineers originated from their home in the constellation of the Pleiades and visited our planet millions of years ago from a base on Venus. These powerful creator beings came to Earth with the intention of beginning a well-designed, scientific plan to fashion a species that would eventually evolve to the intellectual level of the star travelers who had created them.

Incredible Skeletal Remains Scattered around World

However one may accept the provocative theories of Dr. Cabrera and the controversial evidence of his thousands of petroglyphs, there have been some astonishing skeletal remains unearthed throughout our planet. In the United States alone, archaeological digs have produced skeletons of primitive men and women over seven feet tall. Hominid remains with horns protruding out of their skulls were found in one burial mound. Other excavations have unearthed giants with double rows of teeth; prehistoric peoples with sharply slanting foreheads and fanged jaws.

And while some scientists marvel over who these forgotten ancient giants might have been, excavations have also been made of unknown humanoid cultures of smaller stature than any known modern pygmy tribes. Such remarkable discoveries might surely cause us to give serious considerations to such theories as those proposed by Dr. Cabrera.

Are We Children of the Earth--or of the Stars?

It has always seemed logical that we should know a great deal more about who we really are as a species before we begin to explore other worlds. For one thing, it seems that we humans are much older than the scholars of previous generations believed us to be. Even the most orthodox of our scientists keep working to push back the official age of *Homo sapiens* and the earliest ancestors of our species.

The May 7, 1998 issue of the British journal *Nature* presented the work of a group of scientists who assert that the fossils they discovered in Kenya in 1995 represent the earliest known of our ancestors to be able to walk erect. Tests confirmed that the fossils were about 4.07 to 4.12 million years old, thus pushing back the emergence of bipeds more than 500,000 years.

On June 4, 1998, Italian scientists conducting excavations in east Africa announced their discovery of a million-year-old skull that displayed specific human characteristics. Such a find suggests that *Homo sapiens* was beginning to evolve out of earlier hominid forms as early as 1.1 or 1.2 million years ago, 300,000 years earlier than had previously been thought. Italian paleontologist Ernesto Abbate contends that over the last five million years as many as 20 different species of human have existed.

Examining the Skulls of Three Incredible Entities

Step in a museum in Cusco, Peru, and you will clearly see evidence of three different species of evolving humanity.

To our knowledge no scientists have examined these skulls and pronounced any official designations as to their origins, so we will name the first skull the "Conehead Humanoid."

Bigger, thicker, longer than the false skulls worn by the comedic trio of Jane Curtin, Lorraine Newman, and Dan Akyroyd on *Saturday Night Live*, this skull is greatly elongated and by contemporary standards has extremely large eye sockets. Of course we are aware that certain primitive cultures practiced binding the skulls of newborn to produce elongated skulls, but these skulls appear otherworldly and alien to our species.

And speaking of otherworldly, in a nearby display case is a skull that is so incredibly large and unbelievably round that we will name it the "Bowling Ball-Skulled Humanoid."

This skull has enormous eye sockets. If this was truly a primitive human species, then they had a brain capacity about two times that of ours. It is difficult not to envision this skull belonging to the species of alleged extraterrestrial visitors that some UFO researchers have named the "Grays," a seemingly reptilian species with unusually large skulls and eye sockets.

Continuing in our examination of the skulls gathered in this museum, there is no way to prepare for the presence of the most astonishing noggin of all, the one we have nicknamed, "Double Brain."

This skull actually appears to be a double hemisphere, as if left and right brain each had a portion of an expanded cranium. If this skull is, indeed, human or humanoid, then its possessor had a brain capacity more than twice our own. Again, it is difficult to examine this skull and not remember some of the sketches of extraterrestrials made by UFO contactees and abductees.

Even our most hard-nosed scientists can see that human evolution had more stops, starts, and dead ends than the old theories and textbooks had allowed. But these three skulls in a Peruvian museum—especially the latter two described—seem to be biological impossibilities by all that we understand about our own human realities. At this time, the largest human skull documented in medical literature had a cranial capacity of 1,980 ccm—and its shape was normal in every way. The abnormally round skull with the enormous eye sockets and the bizarre double hemisphere skull would easily boast a cranial capacity over 3,000 ccm.

With such mute evidence as those bizarre skulls in Peru and the weird skeletal remains of horned giants and miniature people in the United States, it seems at least a viable hypothesis that our species may well have had a few evolutionary boosts from some genetic engineers from elsewhere.

The Descent of the Super Beings from Nibriu

Beginning with his challenging *The Twelfth Planet*, Zecharia Sitchin has written a number of books detailing the creation stories of the people of Sumer, the first human civilization documented by our conventional historical records.

Sitchin's hypothesis is that a species of super-beings from the planet Nibriu visits our solar system every 3600 years; and it was during one of these cyclical visits 400,000 years ago that they colonized Earth. Then, about 200,000 years ago, their genetic engineers developed Homo sapiens from the more primitive related species of Neanderthal.

In July 1997, a prominent research team established quite conclusively that the mitochondrial DNA of Neanderthals was so distinct from that of our species that it is most unlikely that humans descended from them. Sitchin and others agree that Neanderthal did not lead to *Homo sapiens* through evolution, but through genetic engineering by super-scientists from the stars.

Tracing Modern Man Back to "Chance DNA" Mutation

Conventional scientists, tracing modern humans back to a common founding population in Africa about 150,000 years ago, have discovered the origin of a genetic feature that sets modern humans apart from our prehistoric ancestors—the modern male sex chromosome. In December 1997, Peter Underhill told the American Society for Human Genetics that the modern Y chromosome, the element in DNA that turns an embryo into a male, diverged from its predecessors due to a chance DNA mutation.

While we may ponder exactly what—or who—provoked that "chance mutation," scientists affirm that the newer variant involved the substitution of one biochemical for another on the DNA ladder that forms the Y chromosome. This mutation produced an "Adam" whose offspring bore enough sons to create a new branch of humanity, leaving the old to wither and dwindle to borderline extinction. This was possible, the scientists claim, because at the time there were only around 5000 humans on Earth.

DNA Pioneer Speculates Humans Seeded Here

Such an assertion of the "chance DNA mutation" that suddenly caused the upward evolutionary spiral to create our modern species of humankind brought to mind the remarkable statement made by Dr. Francis Crick, co-discoverer of DNA. He stated in 1971 that the uniformity of the genetic code made it appear as though life passed through a very narrow bottleneck, so narrow that one could easily assume that our species began with one set of parents.

In addition, Dr. Crick speculated, sufficient time had elapsed in the solar system to allow life to have evolved twice. That is, a civilization capable of sending out rockets could already have come into existence and sent "creatures like ourselves" to Earth to plant the seeds of life. Indeed, Dr. Crick stated, our own scientists might be seeding faraway planets a thousand or two thousand years from now.

In terms of our origin as a species, there is a general consensus, at least among our more unorthodox theorists, that humans did not derive from apes—suddenly or slowly—and it is of little significance that the chimpanzee and the human being share 98% of similar DNA.

After all, the genes of the dolphin, the congenial marine mammal, are also amazingly similar to our own. Researchers at Texas A&M University stated in August 1998 that 13 out of 22 dolphin chromosomes are exactly the same as ours. In fact, fossil evidence indicates that 30 million years ago the dolphin had more brainpower than did the ancestors of modern humans.

Following Conventional Origin Theories Difficult

Even if we attempt to keep peace with more conventional theories of human origin, we are left facing so many mysteries that as yet have no sensible kind of conventional solution.

For example, throughout the American Southwest and in other places around the world, humanoid footprints, sandalprints, and shoeprints have been found in geologic strata indicative of 250 million years old.

What bipedal creatures with humanlike feet were walking around on those sandy beaches of the Pennsylvanian Period of the Paleozoic Era? This was the age of the amphibians. Have we missed two-legged, shod bipedal amphibians somewhere in the fossil record?

In Pershing County, Nevada, a shoe print was found in Triassic limestone, strata indicative of 400 million years, in which the fossilized evidence clearly revealed finely wrought double-stitching in the seams.

Carved bones, engraved stones, together with what would appear to be ornamental coins have been brought up from great depths during well-drilling operations.

A strange, imprinted slab was found in a coal mine. The artifact was decorated with diamond-shaped squares with the face of an elderly man in each box.

Smooth, polished concrete blocks forming a solid wall were found in a coal mine. In other coal mine discoveries, pots, pans, eating utensils—even a gold necklace—have been dislodged from lumps of coal.

A metal spike was found in a silver mine in Peru.

A metal, bell-shaped vessel, inlaid with a silver floral design, was blasted out of solid rock near Dorchester, Massachusetts.

When what appeared to be an ordinary geode was picked up by rock hunters near Olancha, California, and cut in half, the interior revealed a concretion formed around an object of hard, shiny metal and what looks like porcelain. X-rays of the concretion show an obviously artificial device sealed within and appears very similar to a contemporary spark plug. If the fossil shells encrusting the geode's surface are at least half a million years old, then how much older must be the device contained within?

When Brad asked an archaeologist friend about such matters as the above, he was surprised to hear the other man admit he was aware of many such anomalous finds. The problem, he commented, is that as scientists

> we cannot work with such anomalies as 500,000 year-old sparkplugs. We must have the entire technological site to go with it. We must dig up the rusted automobile and the ruins of the gas station and split-level house in order to make any kind of official announcement of such bizarre, out-of-time artifacts.

Could Future Time Travelers Have Left These Artifacts?

The operative word in such puzzlers is *time*. Conventional archaeologists would jeopardize their careers if they admitted knowledge of such impossible discoveries. Time travel could provide us with a more suitable answer to some of these archaeological anomalies than ancient civilizations. One could argue that such finds are just too sporadic, too scattered to be the product of any full-scale civilization. Maybe time travelers from our future dropped some of these objects when they were returning to view the ancient and prehistoric history of Earth.

It is at least theoretical that time travelers from our Future are purposely placing such artifacts in our Past so that we may find them in our Present and be provoked to research more ambitiously our human origins.

For example, every good farmer knows that corn, the great New World Native American contribution to the food stores of Earth, requires the hands of humans to cross-pollinate. Experts declare that at 9,000 years, corn is our oldest domesticated seed crop. How then can we explain the 80,000 year-old Mexican corn pollen that was brought up by a Humble Oil Company drill?

And talking about evolutionary stops and starts, who were the mysterious Mullion people? This culture suddenly appeared approximately 10,000 years ago along the Algerian coast with the largest skeletal population in the entire prehistoric record. In addition, the Mullions also possessed the largest cranial capacity of any population the world has ever known—approximately 2,000 cc versus our present 1,400 cc.

Whoever they were, the Mullions inhabited the site only briefly, and their population appeared to consist mostly of women and children, who worked with tool types and domesticated animals never before seen.

"There's No Such Thing as Macroevolution"

Lloyd Pye, author of *Everything You Know Is Wrong*, writes that there is no such thing as macroevolution:

> There is no trace of it in the fossil record or in the world around us. Sea worms did not and do not become fishes; fishes did not and do not become amphibians; amphibians did not and do not become mammals. In every case the difference between critical body parts and functions (internal organs, digestive tracts, reproductive systems, etc.) are so vast, transition from one to another would require dramatic changes that would easily be discernible in the fossil record.

Perhaps a living example of the point that Pye is making would be the coelacanth, a marine creature thought to be extinct for at least 80 million years that keeps showing up in the nets of fishermen. Until a specimen of that rather grotesque fish with four fleshly fins resembling stubby legs was swept up by fishermen near Madagascar in 1938, paleontologists only knew the coelacanth as a fossil from the ages of the dinosaur. The most recent specimen was found in an Indonesian fish market in the summer of 1998—and the coelacanth remains unchanged for well over 100 million years. It displays no evidence of evolving into a crocodile or a dolphin or anything else.

If macroevolution doesn't provide us with the great sweeping answers of planetary existence, then we must settle for microevolution. As Lloyd Pye explains it, this represents the simplest of modifications, for example, a change in the size or shape of a beak—but not the transformation of gills to wings.

The well-known scientist Stephen Gould created the theory of "punctuated equilibrium," which, as writer Khier Morgan explains,

> really rejects unintentionally Charles Darwin's classic theory of gradual evolution to try to explain what happens after a massive extinction (like an ice age or asteroid impact). They practically join the Creationists by proposing a sudden burst of nature's creativity, producing very different and evolved creatures either from nothing or from leftover form preceding the catastrophe.

As many theorists have suggested, science will never find the so-called "missing link" between apes and humans because it simply does not exist.

To answer the ages-old question of where and how our species originated, Lloyd Pye sets forth three possibilities which echo the consensus of many other theorists:

1) Our ancestors arrived on Earth as part of a planetary migration from an extraterrestrial world.

2) Our progenitors were brought to this planet by an extraterrestrial source that left them here, with or without our ancestors' cooperation.

3) Our species was developed or created by a source that utilized genetic manipulation, crossbreeding, or a combination of both.

The Ancient Astronauts: Godlike But Not Gods

Before we examine the enigma of ancient civilizations that may well have been the creation of these same extraterrestrial scientists and engineers, we should point out one thing. To theorize that our human species may have received some alien genetic boosts that accelerated our progress on our evolutionary trek is *not* to grant these ancient cosmonauts with divinity. Although our more primitive ancestors may have deemed these star visitors as angelic or godlike, there is no reason for us to confuse these beings with the Supreme Creator of the Universe.

If our species was genetically altered in its prehistory—and an increasing amount of physical evidence indicates that this possibility certainly does exist—then those extraterrestrial or multidimensional scientists were physical, rather than ethereal. These entities accomplished feats of their advanced technology that our own scientists may likewise achieve on other worlds some day in the future.

Space Dust and the Seeding of Life on Earth

For years now, scientists have pretty much agreed that the basic building blocks of life on Earth came from the stars. In July 1998, Jeremy Bailey of the Anglo-Australian Observatory in New South Wales, Australia, said that he and his colleagues have found more evidence that space dust provided the seeds for life on Earth and that a prehistoric warm, volcanic environment supplied the incubator.

For evolutionary scientists, one of the great riddles in the origin of life is how amino acids and peptides became activated in primordial conditions. Reporting in the journal *Science*, Claudia Huber and Gunter Wachtershauser of Technische University in Munich believe they have the answer.

The researchers mimicked the conditions that would have existed deep in the ocean near volcanic vents. They heated amino acids to the boiling point in the presence of gases found in volcanic conditions. The result was the formation of peptides, the next step in building life, which lies intermediate between an amino acid and a protein.

The Bottom Line: We Are All Star Stuff

Genetic engineers from an extraterrestrial world or not, we are star stuff and our molecular home is somewhere out there in space.

Perhaps a plaque at the National Air and Space Museum, Smithsonian Institution, Washington, D.C. says it simpler and more poetically:

> Stars are the ancestral well of the universe. In the turbulent lifetimes of millions of stars, matter has been forged in the explosive transaction with energy. Oxygen, carbon, nitrogen; gasses, liquids, and solids; almost all the natural elements are born in the stars.

> ...We ourselves are made of star matter. We are the matter of the universe itself—combined in new shapes—struggling to comprehend its origins, its symmetry, and its destiny. Studying the stars is both a curiosity about the unknown and the molecular longing for home.

> The stars guard the answers to our mysteries: they hold the keys to both the future and the past.

> And among the stars, we may not be alone.

THREE

THE ENIGMA OF ANCIENT CIVILIZATIONS

There it stands before you, the Great Pyramid of Giza—the stuff of which legends, dreams, and alternate states of reality are fashioned. At last you are really here, standing before it, beholding its awesome presence as if it is an archetype from the unconscious that has suddenly manifested in the ancient desert sands of Egypt. Inspired lines of poetry, the tributes of emperors and kings, the awe-struck journals of early explorers, and the cinematic efforts of a dozen epics have all attempted to pay adequate tribute to this most magnificent of structures.

If you allow your psyche to open fully to the experience, you will no doubt feel at one with a thousand or more vibrations of those who have entered these stone portals before you.

And yes! It is really you going inside the Great Pyramid! You are actually doing it yourself—not vicariously allowing Charlton Heston, Harrison Ford, Cecil B. DeMille or Steven Spielberg to do it for you.

But you do not simply walk into the King's Chamber. You climb—crawl really—on a steep incline through a very small tunnel slanting upward for at least a hundred yards. Then you emerge into a larger chamber in which, you are relieved to note you can once again stand upright. But the climb isn't over. You have even steeper steps to surmount until you at last enter the King's Chamber.

If you expect a movie-set tomb when you enter the chamber, you will be disappointed. All the glorious golden artifacts and the mummies were removed a long time ago. All that remains is this vast bare room with a large, open sarcophagus at one end.

Echoes of the Ages in the Pharaoh's Sarcophagus

Art had quite an amazing experience when he lay down within the sarcophagus:

> I don't know what got into me, but after a long climb to the King's Chamber, I took one look at the giant sarcophagus and I knew that I wanted to do what most people couldn't. What would it be like to be inside an ancient Egyptian coffin, to feel the presence of thousands of years—to lie down with kings in the middle of the oldest, largest structure in the world? I wasn't prepared for the experience.
>
> First of all, you have to understand that the Great Pyramid at Giza is not just any structure. We'd already been to Greece and seen the

Parthenon, one of the pinnacles of human achievement in architecture and design. But to put it simply, Giza is from another world entirely. In fact, how and why it was constructed is one of the world's great puzzles.

Mathematically, the Giza Pyramid is laid out based on geographical information that no human being could have possibly had at that time. For example, according to John Zajac, it is placed in the direct center of Earth's landmass, both in longitude and latitude. This would require intimate knowledge of Africa, Europe, and the new worlds. Including the entire planet, the average height of land above sea level (as can be measured only by modern satellite) is 5,449 inches—the exact height of the Great Pyramid.

But there's something even more fantastic. Zajac tells us that, mathematically, the construction of the pyramid's inner tunnels and chambers duplicates major religious events in human history, including the Jewish Exodus and the birth and death of Jesus.

Was the Great Pyramid based on spiritual knowledge? Could the necessary information to construct the pyramid have been supplied by extraterrestrials? Who knows? We only know that it is truly the most amazing, so-called 'human structure,' bigger than thirty Empire State Buildings. And there I am—deep inside it, right in the Kings Chamber, stepping into the giant stone sarcophagus of the pharaohs.

As I lay down in the coffin what I experienced was something I will never forget. It was not the echo of my voice as I spoke from the sarcophagus, but the vibrations that I felt when I spoke. It was as if my voice became the Voice of the Ages, as if somehow an ancient coffin made of cold stone had come to life. I could feel what 'Egyptians' from almost 5,000 years ago must have experienced as they placed the giant coffin in the room—which is at the center of the giant pyramid.

I smelled the damp, musty odor of the coffin; and I thought of the hugeness of the stone monument in which I was encapsulated. It was truly hard to imagine the centuries of darkness endured by that room. As I lay there, I felt very small and very human—and very awake. Talk about a feeling of self-awareness.

The Message of the Great Pyramid

John Zajac once gave *Dreamland* listeners a guided tour of the Great Pyramid after which he concluded that:

Clearly, whoever built the Pyramid had access to information beyond that which earthlings possessed at that time—at least earthlings as we know them. Now, one can argue that we were visited by scientifically advanced beings from outer space who [sic] taught us their technology...If so, these advanced beings had the paramount goal of leaving behind a message that would endure for eons.

...The message would have to be universal yet simple, survive the centuries, and be understood by all the Earth's inhabitants despite language and cultural differences.... So far the message indicates that whoever built the pyramid knew the Earth well: the length of the year, the radius of curvature, the standard measurement techniques, the average height of the continents, and the center of the landmass. They were able to construct something that we still cannot construct today, and they were able to tie all these things together in this single structure.

A Mysterious Sound Fills the King's Chamber

Brad described an eerie phenomenon of an entirely different nature that occurred when he visited the King's Chamber:

Since we were standing in what is probably the single most mystical pilgrimage point for metaphysicians on the entire planet, I felt compelled to lead a very brief creative visualization of a possible past life that our souls might have experienced in ancient Egypt.

Afterward, when I turned to touch the right forefinger of the person next to me, a strange, high-pitched sound filled the King's Chamber. All around me I noticed members of the group uncomfortably turning their heads and scrunching their shoulders toward their ears.

How would I describe the sound? If you saw *2001: A Space Odyssey*, you couldn't forget the piercing sound the monolith made when it was uncovered on the Moon and beamed its signal toward Jupiter. You may have noticed a similar sound in *E.T. the Extraterrestrial*, when E.T. touches his right forefinger to Elliot's right forefinger.

Always the researcher as well as the participant, I methodically checked each of the half-dozen tape recorders in the chamber. I put my ear to the single dim electrical bulb that provided the only source of illumination in the chamber. None of the camera batteries or recorders were emitting anything other than their normal soft clicks and buzzes. The loud, piercing sound was not coming from anywhere in particular. It was coming from all around us.

Later, we discussed the manifestation back in our hotel. Some of the members of our tour group believed that the sound that we had heard had been directed toward us as a means of attuning our level of awareness more completely to the vibrations necessary for contact with higher intelligences, multidimensional beings of Love and Light. It seemed to many to be a convincing sign of confirmation that each of us had heard the same sound at the same time in a place where no such sound should have been.

Sadly, the experience had proved too intense for one of the members of our group, and it seemed as though she had literally disappeared from our midst in the King's Chamber after the sound had manifested. Even hours after we had exited the Great Pyramid, there was no trace of her. No one saw her leave the King's Chamber and we were all baffled as to what could have happened. Thankfully, the woman had been found later wandering the streets of Cairo in a disoriented state of mind and had been taken to the home of a kind Egyptian family until she was able to contact the proper authorities and be returned to our group.

Visiting Sacred, Holy, and Mysterious Sites

There is no question that such powerful places as the Great Pyramid have strange and mysterious effects upon those pilgrims who visit these sacred and significant sites. And there is no telling what incredible discoveries will be made in the next few years that will link our past to our future in ways not yet dreamed of by the average man or woman.

Somehow these great monuments and ancient city sites are connected with the mysteries of what elements comprise the true nature of Time and who we as a species truly are. And for those of us who seek the Source of paranormal phenomena, we are driven to explore the sacred sites and holy places of the Earth for clues to the origin of our deepest and most profound enigmas.

Mysterious phenomena that run the gamut from the appearance of UFOs to the manifestations of spirit beings have been widely reported in many places: the Sphinx, the Great Pyramid of Giza, and Luxor in Egypt; Masada, Qumran, and Jerusalem in Israel; the ancient Nabatean city of Petra in Jordan; Machu Picchu, Ollantaytambo, and Sacsahuaman in Peru; Tiahuanaco in Bolivia; and the red rock vortexes of Sedona, Arizona.

Why are these areas so revered? Did the ancients sense that certain physical locations contained somehow within themselves a power that encouraged the realization of prayers, meditation, and altered states of consciousness? Perhaps there are electromagnetic frequencies at work here. Or other energies not yet identified by our sciences that literally open a doorway between dimensions.

Interestingly, if one were to conduct an excavation beneath the great cathedrals, churches, and synagogues of Europe, one would find the even older remains of a place of worship cherished by ancient practitioners of the Old Religion. If one were to conduct similar digs beneath the great cathedrals, churches, and synagogues of North and South America, one would be likely to find evidence that the grounds on which they were constructed were considered sacred and holy by the native people of the region.

Perhaps the ruins of great cities of lost civilizations around the planet are considered sacred because of memories within the collective unconscious of *Homo sapiens* that cherish the presence of the mysterious master builders from elsewhere who constructed such magnificent tributes to a dimly remembered past.

The Wonders of the City of the Dead

When the Incas were a flourishing empire over 600 years ago, the remains of a great city they named Tiahuanaco, "the City of the Dead," were already considered ancient. Bits of pottery and other artifacts indicate that the city may be at least 20,000 years old. Some authorities double that date and point out that the high plateau on which it rests had once been much closer to sea level than its present altitude of 13,000 feet. If this is so, then what known terrestrial civilization was capable of constructing massive stone cities 40,000 years ago?

The Calassassayax (house of worship) at Tiahuanaco is so similar to the Egyptian temple of Karnak in design and layout that its relative dimensions make it almost a scale model of the Old World structure. Were the two ancient cities built by the same mysterious people?

The Impossible Ancient City of Sacsahuaman

Many of the stones used in the construction of the ancient Peruvian city of Sacsahuaman are thousands of tons in weight. To say, as conventional historians do, that the historical Incas constructed this city for giants is to grant them superhuman powers. The quarries that yielded the huge stones for Sacsahuaman are located nine to twenty miles away. Some of the blocks that have been neatly fitted into place weigh as much as 200 tons, and the largest is twelve feet thick and twenty-five feet tall. No two blocks are alike, and they all fit together so perfectly and so precisely that a mechanic's thickness gauge cannot be inserted between the rocks. And all this without using an ounce of cement.

No matter how sophisticated the Inca may have been in certain areas of human endeavor, how could a primitive people that didn't even have the wheel haul such gargantuan boulders over twenty miles up a mountain side to construct the massive, sprawling city? Even our most modern earth-moving machinery in the 1990s would be dwarfed by 200-ton blocks of stone, and our most skilled engineers would be hard-pressed to duplicate the giant mountain fortress of Sacsahuaman.

Who Were the Mentors of the Ancient Egyptians?

Egyptian hieroglyphs, considered to be the oldest written records of humankind, reveal that Egyptian children were taught that the world was round more than 3,600 years before Columbus set sail under the aegis of the Spanish crown to prove that same fact to a doubting Europe. Egyptian students were given a curriculum of history, astronomy, medicine, engineering, agriculture, and the household arts. They were also tutored in a highly developed legal system and a moral and religious philosophy.

There is a strange paradox soon discovered when studying Egyptian history. It would appear that the civilization began at its peak and worked its way downward. If this is so, the question comes at once to mind: who taught the ancient Egyptians an academic curriculum that could not have been equaled in 15th century Europe?

The Apkallu Create an Instant Advanced Civilization in Mesopotamia

The Sumerians of ancient Mesopotamia made no secret of the teachers who 6000 years ago, within an impossibly brief period of time, transformed them from primitive tribespeople to the inhabitants of a remarkable city-state. Their teachers were the Apkallu, and their principal leader was Oannes, the "beast with reason," who had a body that resembled that of a great fish and a head that combined the features of fish and human.

Oannes and his kind had descended in a star and transformed the Sumerians, who had been living "like beasts in the field, with no order or rule," into instant experts in metals, ceramics, and hundreds of other skills. Where before only crude huts and tents had stood, there now arose permanent homes, temples, towers, and pyramids. The Sumerians under the tutelage of Oannes gave the world the first love song, the first school system, the first directory of pharmaceutical concoctions, a law code, and the first parliament.

The origins of Western culture were born in Sumer. The roots of the Judeo-Christian religious belief structures bloomed forth from the "tree of knowledge," the Garden of Eden, that tradition places in that same area.

At the height of the Greek civilization, the highest known number was 10,000. After that sum had been attained, the Greek mathematicians could only fall back on "infinity." Centuries before the Greeks, the Sumerians had achieved remarkable accomplishments in mathematics. A tablet found in the Kuynjik hills contained a 15-digit number—195,955,200,000,000.

Whoever Oannes and the Apkallu really were, according to the ancient writers and the oldest of tradition, the only purpose of these "strange creatures" was to instruct humankind in the ways of civilization.

Recent Exciting Archaeological Discoveries

On January 18, 1998, the Egyptian museum in Cairo put on display an ancient metal statue that had been cast more than 4,000 years ago for Pharaoh Pepi I, ruler of the Sixth Dynasty. Egyptian and German archaeologists put a year and a half of work into restoring the statue and declared it not only a rare piece of art because it was made of hammered copper, but pronounced it one of the world's oldest known metal statues.

In March 1998, Reuters news service reported the find of a richly colored wall fresco, dated about 2,000 years old, that appears to be a panoramic view of ancient Rome from the air.

On April 26, 1998, the *London Times* carried the story of the discovery of buildings found underwater off the coast of Japan that had been constructed over 8,000 years ago by a previously unknown civilization with a high degree of technology.

Now What About the Secret Chamber in the Sphinx?

Such announcements are exciting in themselves, and we delight in the release of more information about some of the remarkable artifacts being unearthed each year in archaeological digs, but pardon us, what about the secret chamber in the Sphinx? Or the tunnel that ancient tradition hints exists between the Great Pyramid and the Sphinx?

And, in the final analysis, was the Great Pyramid simply a burial place for pharaohs, or was it a place of initiation for those members of a secret priest craft?

Gregg Braden, author of *Awakening to Zero Point: The Collective Initiation* and *Walking Between the Worlds: The Science of Compassion*, asserts that the pyramids and the Sphinx offered ancient initiates the "opportunity of simulation of various vibrations," aspects of fear that were recreated in pyramidal chambers. The Egyptian initiates and students of ancient mysticism would enter a certain chamber to learn to overcome self-doubt or jealousy or anger, and so forth.

In the 1930s and '40s, America's most astonishing prophet, Edgar Cayce, said in psychic readings that around the year 1998 a hidden "Hall of Records" would be found beneath the right paw of the Sphinx, which sits among the famous pyramids on Egypt's Giza plateau.

In their book, *The Message of the Sphinx*, Graham Hancock and Robert Bauval state that such a chamber of nine rooms has been found, but that the Egyptian government continues to keep this reality under tight wraps. To substantiate their claims, Hancock and Bauval insist that classified high-tech radar photographs taken from a 1994 NASA shuttle confirm the existence of the chamber.

Hancock and Bauval believe that the Sphinx was not built by the pharaohs of Cheops' time, circa 2600 BCE, but by extraterrestrials as long ago as 10,500 BCE. If this much older date can be established, as Hancock commented, "a paradigm shift of stunning proportions would be necessary."

Hancock and Bauval believe the opening of the secret chambers has been delayed by Egyptian officials for three basic reasons:

1. Islamic fundamentalists may bring down the Egyptian government if it appears that Western influence appears to be growing, especially if secrets unveiled from the Sphinx should contradict what they hold to be holy knowledge.

2. Jewish leaders are reluctant to explore the mystery because they, too, may not welcome facts that could establish a prior civilization.

3. Christian leaders, as well, may fear that the orthodox story of creation could be challenged by messages that were kept secret by the Sphinx.

Did the Ancient Egyptians Have Airplanes?

In 1969, Dr. Kahlil Messiha did not find it necessary to enter a secret chamber when he found evidence to indicate that the ancient Egyptians had flying machines as early as the third or fourth century BCE. He discovered the model of an airplane or a glider in a dusty box of bird models in a storeroom of the Cairo Museum.

So how did Dr. Messiha conclude that this object was an aeronautical model and not simply a representation of a bird? Most of the bird figures found at excavations in Egypt are half-human, half-bird in design, but this model was very different. It appeared to be a representation of a high-winged monoplane with a heart-shaped fuselage that assumed a compressed ellipse toward the tail.

The object, constructed of sycamore, actually bears a striking resemblance to the American Hercules transport plane, which has a distinctive wing shape. Dr. Messiha's brother, a flight engineer, agreed with him and added that the airfoil shape of the model demonstrates a "drag effect," evolved comparatively recently in the field of aeronautical research.

The tail of the model was really the most interesting aspect of the object. "It has a vertical fin," Dr. Messiha commented. "There is no known bird that flies equipped with a rudder."

In addition, all the bird figures discovered in Egyptian excavations are lavishly decorated and have been fitted for legs. The model of the aircraft has no legs and only a very faint trace of an eye painted on one side.

Neither is the object a toy. Dr. Messiha stated firmly that the model was too scientifically designed and it required a great deal of skill to make it.

The ancient Egyptian engineers always made models of things in their contemporary world, Dr. Messiha said, from their funeral boats to their war chariots. We know that funeral boats and chariots existed, because their full-scale versions have been found in addition to their models. In Dr. Messiha's opinion, the airform that he discovered in a box of relics excavated at Saqqara in 1898 is a scale model of a full-sized ancient Egyptian flying machine of some kind.

The Hall of Past, Present and Future in the Temple Seti I

In an interview with Art, Gregg Braden spoke of the temple called Seti I in Abydos, Egypt, that contains a chamber named the Hall of Past, Present, and Future. There, on the ceiling, one can observe carvings that appear to be depictions of many products of contemporary technology, such as helicopters, jet airplanes, submarines, and so forth.

While the question remains whether the ancients truly had such technology, were recalling it from an even-more ancient super-civilization, or were viewing the future, Braden maintains that these carvings are just additional indicators that our time is *the time.* In his opinion, the ancient artisans who created the mysterious carving, just as the engineers who built the pyramids and the Sphinx, did so for the benefit of future humankind—that is, us.

Ancient Indian Aircraft for Civilians and Warriors

All this leads us to a discussion of the "vimana." In 1952, G.R. Joyser, director of the International Academy of Sanskrit Research in Mysore, India, declared that Indian manuscripts several thousands of years old explained in detail the construction of various types of aircraft (vimana) for both civil aviation and for warfare. The specific manuscript on aeronautics contained eight chapters and included plans for the construction of aircraft that traveled in the air, moved under water, or floated pontoon-like on the water's surface. The ancient vimanas were fully equipped with cameras, radio, and a kind of radar system.

The *Vymanika Shastra* consists of nearly 6,000 lines, or 3,000 verses, dealing specifically with the construction of airplanes. The work is attributed to Maharashi Bharadwaja, a Hindu sage, who begins by making obeisance to the Divine Being, "who is visible on the crest of the Vedas, who is the fountain of the eternal bliss, and whose abode is reached by vimanas or aeroplanes."

While we're relatively certain that even the most ambitious of our jet pilots have not seriously considered flying to Heaven in their aircraft, perhaps the sage was referring to a being more physical and more accessible than the Supreme Being.

Nuclear Power in Human Prehistory

And perhaps it was aircraft such as the vimana that may have carried nuclear bombs and blasted some cities into dust and fused green glass in prehistoric times.

Indra, a "god being" who bequeathed his name to India, became known as the "fort destroyer" because of the terrible weapons of destruction he carried in his vimana.

Another ancient Indian text, the *Mahabharata*, tells of an attack on an enemy army:

> It was as if...the sun spun around in the heavens. The world shuddered in fever, scorched by the terrible heat of this weapon. Elephants burst into flames...The rivers boiled...Forests collapsed in splintered rows. Horses and chariots were burned up...The corpses of the fallen were mutilated by the terrible heat so they looked other than human....

Fused Green Glass All Over the Planet

Decades ago, when Albion W. Hart, one of the first engineers to graduate from the Massachusetts Institute of Technology, was assigned to a project in the interior of Africa, his party crossed a great expanse of desert. At the time, he was baffled by a large expanse of greenish glass that covered the sands as far as he could see. Later in his life, Hart visited the White Sands area after the first atomic explosion there—and beheld the same type of silica fusion that he had first seen fifty years earlier in the African desert.

Although the modern world did not experience atomic reaction until the 1940s, nuclear power may have been used in a prehistoric war of the worlds. We have physical evidence of this: sand melted into glass in certain desert areas or even the remains of what appear to have been ancient cities destroyed by intense heat. Primitive *Homo sapiens* may have observed such terrible atomic blasts from the shadows of their caves and may well have incorporated such awful acts of destruction into their myths and legends.

There are ancient ruins in Arabia that date back to the time when the southern part of the peninsula was fertile and well watered. In western Arabia there are twenty-eight fields of scorched and scattered stones that cover as many as 7,000 square miles each. These sharp-edged, blackened stones are not volcanic in origin, and they appear to date from the period when Arabia was a lush and fruitful land—that suddenly became scorched into a desert.

Scientists theorize that it was an intense blast of heat, coupled with other catastrophic events that transformed a tropical region of heavy vegetation, abundant rainfall, and several large rivers into the arid wasteland that we know today as the Sahara Desert. Below the parched desert area, excavations have revealed an enormous reservoir of water and soil that once knew the cultivated influence of systematic agriculture.

In the Euphrates valley of southern Iraq, a layer of fused green glass was found that predates the ancient civilization of Sumer. Perhaps the Apkallu had returned to evaluate the possibilities of making a better world utilizing the primitive humans in the area.

Although the Red Chinese have conducted atomic tests near Lob Nor Lake in the Gobi Desert and created their own patches of vitreous sand, there were other large areas of glassy sand in the Gobi which had been recorded thousands of years ago.

The Mojave Desert of the American southwest has large circular or polygonal areas that are coated with a hard substance very much like opaque glass.

There are ancient hill forts and towers in Scotland, Ireland, and England in which the stoneworks have been calcined (changed to an ashy powder by heat). There is no way that lightning could have caused such effects.

One of the oldest cities in the world is thought to be Catal Huyuk in South-central Turkey. Excavations unearthed thick layers of burned brick that had been fused together by such intense heat that the human skeletal remains found among them had been carbonized. All bacterial decay had been halted by tremendous heat.

When a large ziggurat in Babylonia was excavated, it appeared to have been struck by a terrible fire that had split it down to its foundation. In other parts of the ruins, large sections of brickwork had been scorched into a vitrified state. Even large boulders in the vicinity of the ruins had been vitrified.

Examples of such sites as the above continue to provide us with information that leads us to believe that more than the biblical Sodom and Gomorrah exploded so that "the smoke rose up like that from a mighty furnace." References to the destruction of these ancient cities are found in the scriptures of Hindu and Hebrew and in the myths of people as diverse as the Native American and the African. As so many of our leaders appear to ignore the lessons of the known past, we can only pray that we are not doomed to repeat the warnings of a nuclear holocaust in humankind's prehistory.

And what if some great catastrophe should destroy our civilization? What would be left of our mighty United States for archaeologists to excavate 10,000 years from now—or a million years from now?

Not a great deal would remain, for we are builders in timber and steel. We do not construct modern day Machu Picchus, massive cities of stone. The stone buildings that we do have are only thin veneers supported by webs of steel.

In barely more than 2,000 years, our metal vehicles and our railway tracks would be rusted away to misshapen lumps. Our tracts of wooden homes would be splintered bits of mold-covered pulp, and even our once majestic skyscrapers would be reduced to ribbons of red dust blown away by the wind.

And after a few thousand more years, only our great monolithic concrete dams and some scattered pieces of porcelain would remain to bear mute and inconclusive testimony to a once great republic of 250 million people.

FOUR

VISITORS FROM OTHER WORLDS

Recent surveys conducted by reputable national polling organizations reveal that as many as 55% of Americans believe that life exists on other planets.

Certainly in this day and age of astronauts, space shuttles, and Mars landings, it would be quite provincial not to be open-minded enough to entertain at least the possibility that we are not alone in the universe.

But an astonishing 79% of Americans have moved far beyond being open-minded. They believe that extraterrestrials have visited our planet in the last 100 years—and 70% of our citizenry is convinced that our government has been covering up the truth about alien spaceships invading our skies.

A Personal Visit from a UFO

Art and his wife, Ramona need no survey to convince them that something mighty strange is haunting our skies. They might not swear that extraterrestrial aliens are piloting the mysterious aerial objects, but they do know that something unexplained is up there.

Their sighting of an unidentified flying object occurred when the Bells were still working at KDWN and making the 130-mile round trip between Las Vegas and Pahrump. Art relates that

> we were on our way back to Pahrump, and it was about 11:25 pm. About a mile from home, Ramona, who was in the passenger seat, abruptly turned around and exclaimed, "What the hell was that!"
> "I don't know," I said, not having seen anything myself at that point.
>
> Ramona demanded that I stop the car, so I immediately pulled over to the side of the road. It was in the summer when this event had occurred, and although it was late at night, it was blood warm, in the upper 90s. It was also dead quiet. You could hear a cricket at a quarter of a mile. I turned off the engine and got out of the car.
>
> Turning around, looking down the road, I could not believe what I saw. This was a sight that actually stood the hair up on the back of my neck. Hovering over the road and coming up behind us, was this giant, triangular craft. I would estimate that this craft was about 150 feet from

one point of thc triangle to another. It had a strobing red light on the front part of the triangle, and it had two bright, white lights at each point of the triangle. I also believe the craft was above the ground about 150 feet. In a short while, this bizarre craft came directly over our car.

This craft did not fly; it floated. Flying requires aerodynamic support. In other words, a craft has to be going fast enough for air to traverse the wings and support the craft. This thing could not have been going more than 20 miles per hour. And other than perhaps a hang glider, there is nothing that can do that. This thing was operating in apparent defiance of gravity. There was no way of knowing what was moving this craft, because it was silent. Dead silent. It did not appear to have an engine.

Ramona and I stood gazing at this craft until it floated out across Pahrump Valley and disappeared. What did we see? I don't know. I would call this a UFO experience or a Close Encounter of the Second Kind, because we didn't actually meet any aliens or see any or communicate with any in the craft.

Art maintains his objectivity whenever one of his listeners calls in with an account of a UFO sighting, but his own sighting has blunted a good deal of his previous skepticism:

I do not believe that hundreds of thousands of people all around the world have just imagined things or made up reports about such experiences. Thousands of people seeing the same thing cannot all be wrong. I know that Ramona and I did not imagine our experience. It was real.

Granted, there are probably sightings that can be explained as natural phenomena. But there are many others that cannot. And there is something about those many sightings that convince authors in search of a single Source for all the major phenomena on this planet that the UFO enigma plays a very integral role in the Great Mystery.

Did Eisenhower Inspect UFO Crews at Muroc Field?

A most remarkable and controversial story has been circulating in the circuitous corridors of UFO research for forty-six years, and like the alleged crash at Roswell, New Mexico, and despite the debunkers and skeptics, it simply will not go away. According to this account, President Dwight D. Eisenhower, formerly the supreme commander of Allied Forces in Europe, secretly inspected a variety of alien spacecraft assembled at Muroc Field (now Edwards Air Force Base) and communicated with members of their extraterrestrial crews.

An alleged eyewitness of the history-making event, Gerald Light claimed to have traveled to the air base in the company of Franklin Allen of the Hearst newspaper group, Los Angeles Roman Catholic Bishop James McIntyre, and Edwin Nourse of Brookings Institute, President Harry Truman's financial advisor. In an account written by Light on April 16, 1954, he testified that those select representatives of Earth's scientific, political, and religious communities who had been gathered for the secret meeting were in various stages of "collapse and confusion" as each of them realized that their world "had ended with such finality as to beggar description."

During their two-day visit to the air base, Light states that he personally witnessed five separate and distinct types of extraterrestrial vehicles being studied and handled by Air Force officials. Such close inspection was permitted and encouraged by the aliens, whom Light calls, "the Etherians."

Light expressed his conviction that President Eisenhower would make an official declaration to the United States—and the world—regarding the reality of extraterrestrial visitation around the middle of May. Light wrote in his explanation of the event:

> Mental and emotional pandemonium is now shattering the consciousness of hundreds of our scientific "authorities" and all the pundits of the various specialized knowledge that make up our current physics. I watched the pathetic bewilderment of rather brilliant brains struggling to make some sort of rational explanation that would enable them to retain their familiar theories and concepts. I shall never forget those 48 hours at Muroc.

British Pilot Supports Alien Story at Muroc Air Base

UFO buffs cannot seem to forget Gerald Light's two-day visit at the extraterrestrial exposition, either. Arguments wage pro and con whether or not the incident really occurred.

And as so often occurs in UFO research, skeptics of President Eisenhower's legendary secret visit to Muroc seem to have won the field with their claims that it never happened. Then the Earl of Clancarty, a member of Great Britain's House of Lords, declared that he had discovered a British pilot, a gentleman of greatest integrity, who admitted that he had been in attendance on that fateful day in April 1954. He agreed to provide details of the events at Edwards Air Force Base because he believed that all the principals who had been present were now deceased.

According to the pilot, the aliens were able to breathe the air of Earth without any special breathing apparatus and were basically humanlike in their appearance. The essence of their presentation to President Eisenhower and the assembled political and military representatives was that they wished to begin a program of indoctrination for the citizens of Earth that would make all humanity aware of their presence.

Eisenhower feared widespread panic if such a course of action were to be pursued. In his opinion, the people of Earth were simply not mentally or emotionally ready for the revelation that they were not alone in the universe.

The aliens appeared to understand his assessment of the situation, but they informed those present that they would continue to contact isolated humans until the inhabitants of the planet became aware of an extraterrestrial presence.

Apparently, Eisenhower and all the other officials became very uneasy when the aliens demonstrated their incredibly advanced technology including their ability to become invisible.

While the British pilot affirmed that President Eisenhower refused to become a collaborator with the alien agenda, some UFO researchers charge that in the same year (1954), certain covert branches within the

US government and the governments of other super-powers accepted the Etherians' proposition. In effect, they willingly entered a program of world domination, bartering access to certain of Earth's resources in exchange for advanced extraterrestrial technology.

Winston Churchill Ordered Top-Level UFO Probe

On October 18, 1998, *The People* [London] published the details of Sir Winston Churchill's concern over the motives of UFOs when he was Prime Minister of England. In 1952, while reviewing the reports of flying saucers spotted by the Royal Air Force over Germany in 1943, Churchill asked his Air Minister, Lord Cherwell, to investigate the "truth" about the continuing sightings of unidentified flying objects being reported to the War Office.

Such intriguing reports of Churchill's anxiety over a possible alien invasion only recently came to light when the Lord Chancellor, Lord Irvine, admitted the illustrious Prime Minister's concerns and further revealed that the British government continues to hold at least thirty-three files on UFOs classified as top-secret. The information in those files, Lord Irvine said, is so sensitive that it is kept under lock and key at the Public Record Office in Kew, West London. Under questioning by journalists, Lord Irvine conceded that there could be many additional reports in the files of other government departments.

Mysterious MJ-12 Cuts Secret Deal With Aliens

Some UFO researchers accuse a top-secret group of U.S. military and political leaders known as Majestic-12 of ordering the deal cut with the alien intelligences. According to this theory, MJ-12 was formed on September 24, 1947 by special classified order of President Harry S. Truman to clamp a lid of security on all information pertaining to UFOs.

Those investigators who espouse the reality of Majestic-12 affirm that Eisenhower was not unprepared for the sight of the extraterrestrial armada that he viewed at Muroc in April 1954. When he was president-elect, MJ-12 member Admiral Roscoe Hillenkotter briefed him on the saucer crash near Roswell, New Mexico, in which the bodies of four small reptilian entities had been found in July 1947. The Admiral explained how military and civilian witnesses to the downed "flying saucer" had been debriefed and the cover story of a wayward weather balloon had been fabricated to satisfy those journalists and investigators who had been alerted to the initial story that had proclaimed a crashed spaceship.

Even though Eisenhower was aware of the alien presence—as Truman before him—and the cover-up operations of MJ-12, he remained ignorant of the program of cooperation that had been established by the extraterrestrials and the covert government agencies. By far the most heinous of the concessions made to the aliens by the shadow group within the government were the cattle mutilations and the human abductions.

The ETs' explanation for the surreptitious slaughter of cattle was that their dysfunctional digestive systems could best be served while on Earth by sustaining themselves on an enzyme, or hormonal secretion, most readily obtained from various organs in domesticated cattle. They promised that the human abductions would be conducted discreetly and solely for the purpose of their monitoring and better understanding the developing human civilization.

Secret Government Double-Crossed by Alien Agenda

By 1982, even the more optimistic members of the covert government agencies were forced to concede that certain factions of the alien presence had been double-crossing them. For one thing, it was becoming increasingly difficult to ascertain exactly who was in charge of the extraterrestrial contingents. Although still a factor to be reckoned with, the human-appearing Etherians who conducted the demonstration of alien technological might at Muroc in 1954 had been largely supplanted by a smallish group of entities with over-sized skulls, dark buglike eyes, and slate gray complexions. Nicknamed the "Grays," the beings had an overall appearance suggestive of a reptilian heritage.

For another, it appeared that the "discreet" abductions of select humans were producing unusual pregnancies among the female abductees—pregnancies that were most often terminated by the removal of the fetuses in subsequent abductions.

And for yet another, although MJ-12 had created a vast network of underground bases with extensive facilities, it was now evident that the Grays would permit only a limited amount of reverse engineering by human scientists and allowed their extraterrestrial technology to be operated only under their aegis.

The secret government found itself checkmated and outsmarted by the strangers in our skies. Their greed and lust for power had blinded them to clever machinations of the extraterrestrial invaders. Their desire to control the lives and the destiny of their fellow humans had clouded their ability to discern the alien agenda that had been accomplished under their very noses.

According to more conscientious sources within the military and covert agencies, there would have been a mass alien invasion of our planet in 1987 if not for the intervention of a group of benevolent extraterrestrials that forced the Grays to back off from their program of conquest. It appears that the larger body of aliens adhere to the dictum that a planet's biological and technological evolution must not be interfered with in any manner whatsoever. The rogue group of ETs who sought out maverick, self-serving government agencies to barter advanced scientific technology for minerals, water, and human experimental subjects has been warned to cease all interactions with the people of Earth.

If they do not comply, then we may truly witness a war of the worlds with our species and our planet as the spoils of conflict delivered unto the victors to do with as they choose.

What Is the Truth About Alien Invaders?

While some of the above startling assertions have been widely circulated among UFO buffs for the past fifty years, within the last decade we have seen an increasing number of these allegations translated into best-selling books, blockbuster motion pictures, and popular television productions. Concepts and theories that were once the shadowy conjectures of a small number of UFO researchers have become matters of belief for millions of men and women. The frightening specter of alien invasion has burst free from the movie theaters and the television screens and has begun to haunt the minds of an ever-growing audience of true believers.

But how many of the shocking stories of alien abductions, biological experiments on hapless humans, and extraterrestrial scientists working in secret underground UFO bases can be proven to be real events and not simply the creations of paranoid belief structures?

And can it be possible that extraterrestrials have assisted Earth scientists in creating some of our dramatic technological advances since the late 1940s?

High Order of Beings Helps Create Our Space Program

At a press conference in 1954, Dr. Herman Oberth, the German scientist credited as the father of modern rocket technology, startled many by affirming that UFOs were directed by intelligent beings of a very high order, most likely from another solar system, perhaps even another galaxy. He asserted that the spacecraft were propelled by "distorting the gravitational field and converting the gravity into useable energy."

Some years later, shortly before his retirement, when Dr. Oberth was interviewed about the remarkable advances achieved in the field of rocket science, he startled journalists by stating, "We alone cannot take the credit for our record advancement in certain scientific fields. We have been helped." When pressed to identify these "helpers," Dr. Oberth replied, "The people of other worlds."

UFOs Nearby During "Giant Step for Mankind"

According to Russian scientist Dr. Vladimir Azhazha, alien helpers were also on hand during the historic

Moon landing of the Apollo 11 lunar module on July 20, 1969. Soviet intelligence was monitoring the event and heard Neil Armstrong report to Mission Control in Houston that two large UFOs were observing the module as it landed on the lunar surface. Buzz Aldrin stated that he was taking pictures of the alien craft from inside the module to support Armstrong's claim.

Dr. Sergei Bozhich, who also witnessed the Soviet monitoring, said that in his opinion the two UFOs appeared ready to assist the U.S. astronauts in case anything should go wrong with the landing. Once the module appeared to be securely settled on the lunar surface, the alien spacecraft flew away, thus permitting Armstrong to make his "giant step for mankind" without the appearance of otherworldly assistance.

Yet a third Russian scientist, Dr. Alexander Kasantsev, charged that Aldrin's film of the UFOs was censored by NASA officials and was later confiscated by the CIA.

Billions of Taxpayer Dollars In Black Operations

Robert O. Dean insisted that the greatest story in the history of the human race is happening all around us because our government has purposely kept vital information from us for the past 50 years. And if that were not bad enough, Dean points out that $50 billion of our taxes disappear into black budget operations that no ordinary citizen knows exist—because they explore alien phenomena.

Dr. Edgar Mitchell, the Apollo 14 astronaut and sixth man to walk on the Moon is convinced that most of the records for these "black budget programs" have been destroyed. Even if the highest-level government officials were to search for these documents, even if the President or Joint Chiefs of Staff wanted to access this data, "they are going to have a hard time finding it, because it is no longer there."

Dr. Mitchell is convinced that some of the records do exist somewhere, but they would be difficult to locate because they have been moved around over the last 50 years by "persons unknown." In his opinion, there is evidence that points to

> the existence of a faction that operates outside the government and controls much of this information...and it would be almost impossible for the current government to reconstruct anything now.

Top-Secret NATO Document Reveals Alien Monitoring Program

Robert Dean also claimed to have seen a top-secret NATO document entitled *The Assessment: Of A Possible Military Threat to the Allied Forces in Europe* while he served a military tour of duty as an intelligence analyst at Supreme Headquarters Allied Powers Europe (SHAPE) in 1964. According to Dean, the military analysis of the UFO enigma had been prompted because of dramatic events in February 1961.

Although Dean admitted that he had been a UFO skeptic before examining the secret papers, he said that the information contained therein changed his life. Among the records were the details—complete with photographs—of the recovery of twelve alien humanoid bodies from a crashed disk in northern Germany, just about a mile and a half from the Baltic Sea in a little town called Timmensdorfer-strand.

There were close ups of the corpses—beings 3½-4 feet tall, sometimes a little more—and photographs of military personnel dismantling the craft. "The beings had on some kind of little suits," Dean said. "There was fluid in the bodies, but it wasn't like blood. They apparently had lungs and hearts, but those were about the only similarities with human beings."

Dean states that among the conclusions reached by The Assessment were that Earth has been monitored by a number of extraterrestrial civilizations for thousands of years. In the opinion of those experts who evaluated hundreds of UFO reports for NATO, the alien civilizations appear to be peaceful. In truth, they are so advanced that if they were not essentially benevolent, they could have destroyed or enslaved our planet long ago.

In addition to their program of planetary monitoring, the visitors appear to be increasing their contact with humans in a gradual unfolding of a plan that will ultimately result in open contact with Earth's inhabitants.

Based on the large numbers who attest to their own UFO encounters, we are convinced that the sightings have definitely increased in the last couple of decades. But we have to remember that historically the UFO phenomenon has been recorded for several thousand years. As far back as 66 AD, the historian Josephus recorded that people were sighting what they described as "celestial chariots" and "flying shields" in the sky. In the 17th and 18th centuries, people reported "flying ships" in the skies. At the turn of the century, in 1897, people around the world said that they sighted a mysterious "airship" and even conversed with its occupants.

Extraterrestrial, Terrestrial, or Multidimensional?

While we agree with those who assert that Earth appears to be under surveillance by unknown beings that largely fashion what we term the "UFO mystery," we are uncertain whether these entities are of an extraterrestrial origin.

People who share actual experiences with non-human intelligences are not making these things up. The question is not necessarily *whether* these kinds of creatures exist, but the *nature* of such beings.

If we concede that up to 90% of all UFO sightings are misinterpretations of natural phenomena and known terrestrial technology, then we are still left with a possible 10% that may be actual unidentified flying objects piloted by unknown terrestrial or extraterrestrial crews.

Hollywood certainly has not held back in concocting a wide variety of scenarios of possible motives for aliens to visit our planet and to interact with humans. In the late 1940s and early 1950s, the aliens were most often monsters with hostile intentions of conquering Earth.

One of the most impressive exceptions to the nasty "creature features" was Robert Wise's classic *The Day the Earth Stood Still* [1951]. Not only did this give us the cult password, "Klaatu barada nikto," but also the prototype of the calm, compassionate yet firm Space Brother, who warns Earthlings to get their act together or be left to their own self-destructive devices.

In the 1980s, our stellar alien was E.T., the friendly dwarf-sized alien who accidentally found himself stranded on Earth, and was subsequently befriended by ordinary American children. Perhaps one of the more direct movies in terms of addressing an actual meeting with aliens was *Close Encounters of the Third Kind*. Leading man Richard Dreyfuss was drawn to the landing site of a spacecraft containing benevolent occupants. This movie dealt with many of the issues of choosing between the safety of remaining on Earth and the tantalizing curiosity about other life forms and worlds.

On the other hand, the 1996 blockbuster *Independence Day* depicted aliens as horrific and had them arriving in overwhelmingly huge craft, as well as supplying them with intentions of destroying Earth. Our own imaginations—with the generous assistance of Hollywood—have given all of us some idea about what aliens look or act like.

For most people, the idea of alien visitation seems frightening, perhaps thanks to movies such as *Independence Day*. Many other people prefer to believe that visiting aliens would be benevolent and that contact with them would not be a negative experience. In short, they would like aliens to supply us with just what the world needs in these unsettling times.

No Single Answer to UFO Enigma

John W. White, noted author and editor, believes

that no single answer will give us the full story of what UFOs are and where they come from. Some appear to be extraterrestrial vehicles. Others, however, appear to be manifestations of the human unconscious. Yet others appear to be psychokinetically created materializations of light and subtle forms of matter.

Indeed, there may be earth-originated UFOs which may be biological aeroforms native to our upper atmosphere. In addition to possible terrestrial and extraterrestrial UFOs, still others may be extradimensional creatures with craft that materialize into our space-time from other dimensions, other planes of reality.

As we examine the hundreds of UFO cases filed by responsible and intelligent men and women, a larger picture begins to take shape. Obviously, some undeclared, unidentified intelligence has interacted with humankind through our history in an effort to learn more about us, to communicate certain basic concepts to our species, or to guide us in subtle ways to achieve some sort of master plan.

We also sense that there exists some kind of symbiotic relationship between our species and those intelligences we associate with the UFO enigma. While these beings might be—or have been—extraterrestrial in origin, it seems more likely that they enter our world from some other dimension, some other space-time continuum. That being said, then we must acknowledge that these entities might sometimes appear as cosmonauts from space, travelers out of time, eerie ghostlike creatures, or even as angels.

FIVE

ROSWELL AND THE GOVERNMENT
UFO COVER-UP

For years now, controversy has swirled around the alleged occurrences at Roswell, New Mexico in 1947. No one can deny that Roswell has become the Camelot of the UFO buffs, a virtual Flying Saucer Mecca that encourages annual pilgrimages of true believers. Nevertheless, there are many differing opinions about whether it was an alien spaceship, a weather balloon, or a secret Project Mogul balloon that crashed in the desert sixty miles out of town.

What could be more intriguing than the crash of a mysterious craft on a remote ranch northwest of Roswell? And this happened only a week after Kenneth Arnold spotted the nine shiny "flying saucers" flitting across the Seattle sky. With the Roswell crash in early July leading the way, there was an increase of UFO sightings all throughout the summer. Lending even more credibility was the fact that many of these sightings were made by pilots, military personnel, and other trained observers of the sky.

Poll Shows Most Believe Government Hides UFO Knowledge

To commemorate the 50th anniversary of the enigmatic event at Roswell, in July 1997 CNN/Time took a poll that indicated that eight out of ten Americans believe the government is hiding knowledge about the UFO mystery.

In addition, 54% of those surveyed are certain that life exists outside of Earth. Another 35% expect extraterrestrial beings to appear "somewhat" human, and 64% are convinced that alien life forms have made contact with humans; 37% are concerned that ETs are abducting humans, and 37% suspect that aliens have already contacted representatives of the US government.

What Do We *Really* Know About Roswell?

What do we know for certain about the event that happened near Roswell, New Mexico, in July 1947?

We know that on July 8, 1947, Walter Haut, the Public Affairs officer at Roswell Army Airfield sent out a release announcing that the Air Force had "captured" a flying saucer.

The announcement was transmitted to thirty US afternoon newspapers that same day, and the entire nation was electrified with excitement as word spread that a military team had actually recovered debris from the crash site of one of those mysterious airborne discs. After all, people had seen UFOs around the country ever since Kenneth Arnold's encounter with "flying saucers" on June 24.

We also know that the very next day, the press office at the Roswell airfield released a correction of its previous story. It had not been the debris of a flying saucer that had been recovered, after all. It was nothing but the remains of a downed weather balloon.

On July 9, the Roswell Daily Record carried the story of Mac Brazel, the rancher who had found the so-called "saucer," who said that he was sorry that he had told anyone about the crashed junk in the first place. To his eyes it was nothing but "tinfoil, paper, tape, and sticks" stuck together with some "smoky gray" rubber. The whole works only made a bundle about twenty inches long and about eight inches thick. Altogether, the stuff couldn't weigh much more than five pounds.

It may not have been one of those flying saucers, the rancher concluded, but he didn't think it was a weather balloon, either.

Roswell — the Mother of All UFO Conspiracy Theories

For over 50 years now, dozens of UFO researchers have also denied the official account that the rancher, Mac Brazel, found a crashed weather balloon sixty miles outside of Roswell. They believe that he came upon the scattered pieces of a flying saucer, an extraterrestrial spacecraft, and that the military meticulously recovered those pieces—along with its alien crew.

And now we're into the murky, paranoid area of what people believe happened at Roswell and how the story became the Mother of all UFO conspiracy theories.

Over the years, many serious researchers have undertaken extensive investigations to learn more of the truth about Roswell. Despite the fact that the military threatened some witnesses with death, many of those who were involved in the recovery of the crash site have come forward to tell their stories. Others, like Mac Brazel, chose to remain silent, even to their graves.

Such ufologists as nuclear physicist Stanton Friedman, author-researcher William Moore, former military intelligence officer Kevin Randle, and Don Schmitt of the J. Allen Hynek Center for UFO studies, have argued the following points:

- Major Jesse Marcel, the officer ordered to travel to Mac Brazel's ranch and retrieve the remains at the crash site, was an experienced intelligence officer who would be able to identify a downed weather balloon. In 1980, Marcel, long retired, said that his top-security unit had recovered fragments of some strange, weightless material, varying in size from a few inches to three or four feet, some of which bore markings that resembled hieroglyphics.

- Numerous civilians who claimed to have arrived at the crash site remembered seeing the corpses of small, hairless beings with large heads and round, oddly spaced eyes.

- Roswell Army Air Force Base press officer, Walter Haupt, was given direct orders by base commander Colonel William Blanchard to prepare the official press release refuting the flying saucer account. The cover story of the weather balloon initiated the military/government conspiracy to keep the truth of a crashed extraterrestrial UFO from the public.

- One or more of the alien crew may have survived the crash and were shipped along with the debris of their vehicle to Wright Field, thus becoming the residents of the infamous "Hanger 18" at Wright-Patterson.

- A number of civilians were threatened by the military to keep their mouths shut about what really occurred at Roswell. Some were even told that they could disappear and become bleached bones in the desert.

Conspiracy Theories at Staggering Heights of Paranoia

Other Roswell conspiracy theories were not long in surfacing, each one a bit more frightening than its predecessors:

- An extraterrestrial craft did crash at Roswell in 1947, and through reverse engineering of the advanced alien technology at secret airbases such as Area 51, our scientists and engineers have been able to accomplish aeronautical breakthroughs decades ahead of when we might have expected them. Other artifacts found with the crashed extraterrestrial space vehicle were discreetly farmed out to major U.S. corporations who were able to back engineer many technological advances for the benefit of all world citizens.

- One of the aliens of the Roswell crash survived and was kept alive in Hangar 18 at Wright-Patterson Air Force Base. It was through this "extraterrestrial biological entity" (EBE) acting as liaison that a secret agency within the government made secret deals with the aliens, actually exchanging humans for advanced technical data.

• In secret underground military and commercial facilities, aliens have been seen working side by side with earthling scientists and engineers developing additional technological advances derived from extraterrestrial technology. If regular workers should happen to come upon the EBEs, they are reminded of their security oaths and threatened to retain their silence or suffer the consequences.

• In their greedy efforts to gain even more advanced technological data, secret government agencies have allowed aliens to abduct humans and conduct genetic experiments. Alleged witnesses to such activity report subterranean laboratories where the EBEs seek to create part-alien, part-human beings. Others tell horror stories of having observed "large vats with pale meat being agitated in solutions" and large test tubes "with humans in them."

Majestic-12's Advent into the Roswell Mystery Mix

In December 1984, documentary filmmaker Jamie Shandera claimed that he had received a packet in the mail that contained two rolls of undeveloped 35-mm film. Once he developed the film, he discovered what appeared to be a briefing report to President-elect Dwight D. Eisenhower that provided him with the details of the recovery, analysis, and the official cover-up of the 1947 crash outside of Roswell.

Within the report was the description of the four "humanlike beings" that had been found near the wreckage of what had been determined to be a crashed extraterrestrial spacecraft. The secret analysis of the beings acknowledged their humanlike appearance, but concluded that "the biological and evolutionary processes responsible for their development has apparently been quite different from that observed or postulated in *Homo sapiens.*"

From what Shandera could ascertain, some unknown source had leaked the documents to him just a few weeks after the death of the last member of a group of twelve prestigious and top-secret investigators who worked under the code name of "Majestic-12." To help him develop a more complete analysis of the papers, Shandera enlisted the assistance of prominent UFO researchers William Moore and Stanton Friedman.

When the trio released the documents at the 24th Annual National UFO Conference in Burbank, California, in June 1987, they revealed the members of Majestic-12 to be the following:

- Lloyd V. Berkner, known for scientific achievements in the fields of physics and electronics, special assistant to the secretary of state in charge of the Military Assistance Program, executive secretary of what is now known as the Research and Development Board of the National Military Establishment.

- Detley W. Bronk, physiologist and biophysicist of international repute, chairman of the National Research Council, member of the Medical Advisory Board of the Atomic Energy Commission.

- Vannevar Bush, a brilliant scientist, who served from 1947 to 1948 as chairman of Research and Development for the National Military Establishment.

- Gordon Gray, assistant secretary of the Army in 1947, secretary of the Army in 1949.

- Dr. Jerome C. Hansaker, aeronautical scientist and design engineer, chairman of the National Advisory Committee for Aeronautics.

- Robert M. Montague, Sandia base commander, Albuquerque, New Mexico, from July 1947 to February 1951.

- General Nathan F. Twining, commander of the B-29 that dropped the atom bombs on Hiroshima and Nagasaki. In December 1945 he was named commanding general of the Air Material Command at Wright Field. In October 1947 he was appointed commander in chief of the Alaskan Command and later, in 1950, became acting deputy chief of staff for personnel at Air Force headquarters in Washington, D.C.

- Dr. Donald H. Menzel, director of the Harvard Observatory, long acknowledged as a leading authority on the solar chromosphere, co-formulator of the calculations that led to initial radio contact with the Moon in 1946.

- James V. Forrestal, undersecretary, then secretary of the Navy. In 1947, he became Secretary of Defense, coordinating the activities of all U.S. Armed Forces.

• Sidney W. Souers, deputy chief of Naval Intelligence before organizing the Central Intelligence Office in January 1946.

• Hoyt S. Vandenberg, commanding general of the Ninth U.S. Air Force before being named assistant chief of intelligence in 1946. He was appointed the director of Central Intelligence in June 1946.

• Rear Admiral Roscoe H. Hillenkotter, the first director of the Central Intelligence Agency (May 1947 to September 1950), the permanent intelligence agency that evolved from the office organized by Sidney W. Souers.

Pieces of Roswell Crash Debris Surface

On April 10, 1996, Art received a letter from an anonymous source who claimed that his grandfather had been a member of the retrieval team who gathered the crash site debris outside of Roswell in July 1947. The informant claimed to be serving in the military with a security clearance, and since 1974, he had been in possession of his grandfather's souvenir of the Roswell crash, a metallic sample of "pure extract aluminum." He was now bequeathing it to Art.

According to the anonymous informant, the retrieval team had found two dead occupants that had been hurled free of the spacecraft. They also discovered a lone, surviving occupant within the disc-shaped vehicle. The corpses were dispatched to Wright Field. The informant's grandfather was part of the team that accompanied the surviving alien.

Telepathically, the extraterrestrial communicated that his "probe ship," a three-occupant vehicle, had been launched from a larger craft that was stationed at the dimensional gateway to the Terran Solar System, 32 light years from Earth. The aliens had been conducting operations on our planet for over 100 years. Another group was exploring Mars.

The extraterrestrial craft had crashed because it had collided with a meteor while they were in orbit of Earth. The larger craft, a "launch ship," had authorized an attempted soft-landing on the New Mexican desert. Their only option was to activate the "dimensional power plant for deep space travel." To have done so would have opened an energy vortex around the probe ship for 1,500 miles in all directions, thereby destroying large portions of the states of New Mexico, Arizona, California, and sections of Mexico. The three occupants of the probe ship had actually sacrificed their lives rather than destroy the populations with their proximity.

The anonymous informant claimed that his grandfather had spent twenty-six weeks with the team that examined and debriefed the lone survivor of the Roswell crash. The alien being was to be transported to a long-term facility in Washington, D.C., but according to this informant, the aircraft and all aboard disappeared under mysterious and disturbing circumstances while en route.

On April 22, 1996, another letter arrived from the anonymous informant, in which he expressed great disappointment with the negative and closed-minded responses that had been directed toward Art by his listeners when he shared the contents of the previous letter. At the risk of his own court martial, he went on to provide additional information regarding the occupant-survivor of the crash.

Despite a lengthy series of interrogations, the alien refused to disclose any technical information. With his ability to deduce thoughts and questions prior to their being asked, he managed to frustrate his interrogators, which included academic as well as military authorities and consultants from England, France, and Russia.

The probe ship itself was literally dissected, "and it was discovered that the propulsion system had actually fused together the many interior components. There were control-type devices forged in the shape of the alien hand, which were assumed as controls and activation surfaces."

His grandfather told him that what is today fiber-optic technology was a basic aspect of the alien technology within the control panels. There were Westinghouse affiliated persons on the team, and his grandfather always suspected they incorporated such research into the telephone systems.

A few weeks later, the anonymous informant went on to say that as the year 2000 approaches, it is time that the Roswell secret be disclosed:

> Millions have witnessed the UFO phenomena in the last fifty years. Virtually thousands have claimed contact with aliens. What happened at Roswell was a beginning. Not the beginning of the end of civilization, as some feared if the information was disclosed, but actually a beginning of beginnings.
>
> ...Our world is changing. Nothing can stop that...You have the evidence that some have sought and demanded. Discount it or discredit

it.... It matters little in the final analysis.... The truth will come out about Roswell.

The Air Force Debunkers Take Their Turn at Bat

On June 24, 1997, the Pentagon held a special briefing conducted by the U.S. Air Force—timed to coincide with the 50th anniversary of Kenneth Arnold's 1947 sighting of flying saucers—in order to release the Headquarters United States Air Force document, *The Roswell Report: Case Closed.* This publication, stated Col. John Haynes, would be the Air Force's final word concerning 50 years of accusations that the government was hiding evidence of extraterrestrial visitation.

The debris found at the crash site outside of Roswell was from Project Mogul Balloon, a top-secret intelligence gathering device; hence the cover-up was for purposes of national security. The alleged bodies seen around the crash site were not those of extraterrestrial beings or of any living beings. They were actually dummies, roughly the size of humans, used in experiments with high-altitude parachutes that began in 1953.

After the experimental drops, Air Force personnel would retrieve the simulated human forms, and it must have been at certain of these recovery missions that folks around Roswell got the idea that they saw military types picking up "alien" bodies.

Of course there were those who wondered how witnesses could confuse dummies dropped over the desert near Roswell in 1953 with humanoid corpses scattered near a specific crash site in 1947. Colonel Haynes explained this confusion as a manifestation of the mental phenomenon of "time compression." He explained that time compression occurs when your memory melds events separated by many years into "compressed" segments of time.

By this theory, we can interpret that civilians who witnessed the crash site of a weather balloon in 1947 and, six years later, saw Air Force personnel retrieving crash dummies dropped from the skies, recall the two events as one in their compressed memories. And, then, of course, with all the controversy regarding flying saucers and aliens, remember the balloon fragments and the dummies as the debris from a crashed space-craft and the corpses of its extraterrestrial crew.

The Japanese Fugo Balloon Bomb Theory

John A. Keel, veteran ufologist and author, discounts the claims of a crashed spacecraft, as well as the alter-nate U.S. weather balloon and Project Mogul theories. In his opinion, rancher Mac Brazel found the remains of a Japanese Fugo balloon bomb in July 1947. The bizarre alien "hieroglyphics," Keel believes, were simple Japanese instructions, such as "insert in slot B."

The Fugo balloon bombs were part of a very real plan to spread chaos and fear among U.S. citizens during World War II. Constructed of lightweight materials, the balloons crossed the Pacific on the jet stream, a trip that usually took about three days. Remains of the balloons, few of which caused any real damage, were found in over 300 sites throughout the western states from 1943 onward through the next twenty years.

Keel believes that Major Jesse Marcel had no trouble recognizing the debris as anything other than a Fugo bomb, but that ill-informed military officials made rash public statements at the peak of the 1947 flying saucer mania and UFO advocates have carried and exaggerated the story ever since.

Although Keel totally discounts the various Roswell conspiracy theories, he accepts the reality of the UFO phenomenon. He simply does not believe any reports of crashed UFOs, because, as he states it, "UFOs are not crashable."

Roswell as a Red Herring?

Research conducted by Kent Jeffrey definitely threw "ice" on Roswell's "Encounter '97."

In 1993, Jeffrey (an airline pilot and the son of a retired Air Force colonel who knew and worked with General William Blanchard, a key Roswell figure) launched the International Roswell Initiative (IRI). IRI was a grassroots effort to end what so many UFO enthusiasts believed to be a government cover-up of the facts concerning the Roswell event. But his years of subsequent research into the incident brought Jeffrey to a very different conclusion than the supposition with which he had begun.

In the pages of the *MUFON Journal* and other forums, Jeffrey stated that the account of the crash of an extraterrestrial spacecraft outside of Roswell was based on such human mental machinations as "errors in perception, faulty memory, fabricated stories," and "exaggerations and selective presentation of fact." Without a doubt, according to Jeffrey's investigations, "The debris recovered...was that of an ML-307 radar reflector."

While thoroughly discounting the myth of the flying saucer that crashed at Roswell, Jeffrey, like John A. Keel, does not dismiss the reality of the UFO enigma. In fact, he characterizes Roswell as a "red herring, diverting time and resources away from research into the real UFO phenomenon."

For those researchers who will strive to keep the Roswell myth alive and well, Jeffrey challenges them to deal with such questions as the following:

- Why would a machine of such advanced technology simply have broken down and crashed?

- Why would the only wreckage from such a spacecraft be bits and pieces of foil-like material and a few short beams?

- Why would the material from a crashed flying saucer so closely resemble that of the radar reflectors from the balloon array that went down in the area a few weeks earlier?

No Way To Keep Alien Contact Secret

For those who argue that there is no way that any government agency could have kept their secrets regarding visiting aliens or the crash of an extraterrestrial vehicle at Roswell, consider some of the things our government is known to have kept from us.

Would anyone have believed that the government would have deliberately fed children radiation just to see what effect it might have? No, of course not. But Hazel O'Leary, the U.S. Secretary of Energy recently admitted that our government did do such experiments on our children.

Several years ago there was a very rare, incurable, fast-acting, highly contagious Ebola virus that broke out in Reston, Virginia. Did the government tell us about that? They did not.

Suppose there was a comet heading towards Earth, and its collision course was expected to result in the cataclysmic destruction of many of Earth's inhabitants. Would our government tell us? Probably not. Nor would our government tell us if beings from somewhere in the universe came to visit.

Colonel Corso Pumps Up the Mystery

In his provocative and controversial book, *The Day After Roswell*, Colonel Philip J. Corso (U.S. Army, retired) claims that he was given "personal stewardship" of various extraterrestrial artifacts gleaned from the crash of a spacecraft outside of Roswell, New Mexico in July 1947. Corso goes on to assert that he bequeathed the objects of alien technology to various government contractors.

Corso further stated that while the US government has officially denied such an occurrence, they have secretly and ambitiously been reverse engineering as much advanced alien technology as possible. Among the results of such back engineering were fiber optics, light amplification devices, Kevlar (light weight heavily resistant material for use in body armor), and a host of "Star Wars" advances in weaponry.

The late Philip J. Corso, a retired military officer, served his country with loyalty and devotion for many years. He was on General Douglas MacArthur's intelligence staff following the Korean War, and he was later assigned to President Dwight Eisenhower's Security Council, then to the Army Research and Development's Foreign Technology Desk at the Pentagon. We cannot take the testimony of such a man lightly when he declares that the Roswell incident is for real.

According to Corso, the events regarding Roswell went something like this:

> When I moved into the Foreign Technology Division, General Trudeau called me and said, "I'm delivering a file cabinet [of artifacts from the Roswell crash] to you. You go through it and start working up a plan of action and recommendations for me." Trudeau also commented that "this could be bigger than Los Alamos, because we could make space ships light as a feather that could not be penetrated by radiation, cosmic activity, or gunshots."

A German scientist Corso identifies only as "Hans" told him an examination of some of the Roswell material may cause him to "unlearn everything I've ever learned." Corso's reply was, "Hans, you just might have to." One of Corso's first file cabinet discoveries

> was a piece of metal about the size of a postcard. It was paper thin, but the atoms were aligned in it. ...We all failed [to duplicate or back-engineer it]. Those assigned to it thought they were getting close, but it never happened.
> Then we moved on to the integrated circuit...the size of a chip. General Trudeau gave me the instructions to find out who in industry is already working along similar lines, as work on the transistor had already begun in some laboratories.

> Trudeau started a program called "Applied Engineering." We would find people who were work-

ing in a particular area, infuse the technology
through our Research and Development projects,
and we would even fund it. And every time we
thought they were slowing down, we would infuse
a little more [R&D money appropriated by Con-
gress...until they perfected it].

If even the smallest fraction of what Colonel Corso
claims in *The Day After Roswell* could be verified, we
would have one of the most amazing, incredible stories
that you have ever heard in your entire life.

We believe that something important really did happen at Roswell, and our government knows all about it.
We are pretty well convinced there's been a cover-up
about the truth about Roswell.

Former Astronaut Says "Roswell Happened"

On October 25, 1998, John Earls' interview with Dr.
Edgar Mitchell which appeared in *The People* [London]
startled both UFO buffs and skeptics alike when the
former astronaut proclaimed, "Make no mistake, Roswell happened. I've seen secret files which show the
government knew about it, but decided not to tell the
public."

Just a week or so before, Dr. Mitchell had made
some strong statements about the reality of extraterrestrial life forms visiting Earth at a UFO conference in
Connecticut. In the subsequent interview with Earls,
the sixth person to walk on the Moon continued to
shake up the whole field of inquiry regarding the UFO
enigma.

Dr. Mitchell explained that as a scientist and a former astronaut, military people with access to top-secret

files were more willing to speak to him than to civilian researchers with shaky credentials. Admittedly he had begun his inquiries as a cynic, but later he became convinced about the existence of aliens when he began speaking with "the military old-timers" who had been in service at the time of Roswell. The more government documentation he was told about, the more convinced he became.

Dr. Mitchell stated he was shocked to learn the extent to which the UFO mystery had been covered up by the government, but in defense of such actions, he said that there were sound security reasons for not informing the general public the truth about Roswell:

> Quite simply, we wouldn't have known how to deal with the technology of intelligent beings advanced enough to send a craft to Earth. The world would have panicked if we'd known aliens were visiting us.

Dr. Mitchell expressed his belief that those individuals who were in possession of top-secret documentation of alien visitors would soon begin to come forward and that full disclosures will be made within three or four years.

The military people with whom Dr. Mitchell spoke are "tired of the secrecy surrounding Roswell and similar cases, particularly as the information is being leaked."

SIX

ABDUCTIONS & MUTILATIONS: THE SINISTER SIDE OF UFOS

In 1994, Dr. Ron Westrum, an Eastern Michigan University sociologist, helped Dr. Ted G. Goertzel, a sociology professor at Rutgers University, develop a survey designed to reveal if people may have had experiences associated with UFO abductions. The survey, distributed to 697 people chosen at random, consisted of five questions:

Did you ever:
1. Wake up paralyzed with a sense of a strange person or presence in the room?

2. Go through a period in which you apparently lost an hour or more, but couldn't remember why—or where you had been?

3. See unusual lights or balls of light in a room, without knowing what was causing them?

4. Feel that you had actually been flying through the air, although you couldn't recall how or why?

5. Find puzzling scars on your body, but neither you nor anyone else could remember how you got them or where you got them?

If a polled individual responded with a "yes" answer to three questions, the university researchers assessed that he or she had about a 60 percent probability of having been abducted by aliens. Four positive responses would up the percentage to 90 percent. Anyone who answered "yes" to all five is most likely a bona fide UFO abductee.

When Dr. Westrum and Dr. Goertzel determined that 3.4 percent of their survey population gave answers suggestive of an alien abduction, their statistical projections indicated that as many as 8.7 million people may have been taken aboard alien spacecraft.

Transporting nearly nine million unwilling humans aboard extraterrestrial vehicles seems like an incredible task to perform—even for beings with an advanced technology.

Sightings on the Rise

Some years ago, David Webb, an Arlington, Massachusetts, solar physicist, a member of the Mutual UFO Network (MUFON), a respected UFO research organization, presented his estimate that one out of every eight people who had reported seeing UFOs may have been abducted.

Statistical analysis of a precise number based on the "one out of eight" formula would be somewhat difficult to compute since a lot of people claim to see UFOs who are really sighting natural phenomena or conventional aircraft. According to some surveys which report as many as 20 million Americans claiming to have seen a "real" UFO, the Webb Abduction Formula still gives us a lot of people having been kidnapped by UFOnauts.

Why Would the Aliens Want to Examine So Many of Us?

The question that immediately presents itself is why a scientifically advanced extraterrestrial species would need to examine so many Earthlings?

We are all one species, after all, and while individual, pretty much the same in terms of our physical makeup. Would any alien visitors really need to abduct millions of us before they got the picture of what kind of creatures we are?

If the aliens' sinister purposes include the creation of a hybrid species, as so many UFO researchers suggest, then they would no doubt require vast amounts of human eggs and sperm. For years now, the files of certain UFO investigators have been bulging with alleged cases in which women report unusual pregnancies as a very unwelcome aspect of their abduction experience. In a large number of these cases, the pregnancies are terminated by the removal of the fetus in a subsequent abduction.

But what if the aliens are some kind of cosmic Red Cross, inoculating large numbers of our planetary population against some ghastly plague that they, with their advanced science, foresee just around the corner of our time sequence? Perhaps they have absolutely no sinister motives at all. They could just as easily be working to save our species from dying out.

Another theory is that the alien visitors could be "time travelers," our descendents from the distant future returning to study certain negative genetic traits that they now have the capability to refine or to eliminate.

Some researchers make the most disturbing claims regarding the aliens' attempts at crossbreeding or genetically engineering a hybrid species. They accuse a secret branch of the government of having condoned such experiments. It certainly promotes distrust of the government to even consider that some agencies are knowingly turning their backs on a worldwide pattern of abductions being conducted to develop a mutant species of humanoids.

While many scoff at any variation of the alien abduction scenario, UFO investigators such as Budd Hopkins, Whitley Strieber, Dr. David Jacobs, and Dr. John Mack, argue that such UFO abductions are real. At the very least, they believe that men and women around the planet are being regularly and systematically kidnapped by aliens for undetermined purposes. Such accounts have captured the imaginations and provoked dark and terrible fears in large numbers of people.

Abductees Must Have Experienced *Something*

There are literally thousands of accounts of people who have encountered aliens or claim to have actually been taken away by aliens. Many people just choose to laugh the matter of UFO abductions away, without giving any credence to the possibility. But people attesting to abductions or other encounters have seen and experienced something. Just as with the large numbers of UFO sightings worldwide, there are simply too many people reporting alien encounters and abductions for all of them to be hoaxes.

Granted, there are those people who will make things up just for the attention. These folks notwithstanding, we believe there are significant numbers of people who are telling the truth. Now we must attempt to determine exactly what it is that they have seen—and exactly what it is that they have experienced.

Descriptions of UFO Abductors

Although there have been a few reports of alien kidnappers described as standing over six feet tall, in the greatest number of abductions, the UFOnauts are described as about five feet tall and dressed in one-piece, tight-fitting jumpsuits—or in the case of the "Grays," very often no discernable clothing at all.

The complexion of their skin is most often said to be gray or grayish-green and they are seldom described as having any body hair. Their heads appear disproportionately large for their diminutive stature and slight bodies.

Most compelling in the memories of the abductee are the entities' unusually large eyes, most frequently described as black and insect-like, but often said to be snakelike or catlike with slit pupils.

Nearly all abductees describe their captors as having no discernible lips, just straight lines for mouths. Occasionally, an abductee will recall the aliens having made humming or chirping sounds, but communication is generally on what is believed to be a telepathic level.

The alien entities are generally described as having no more than little snubs of noses. In the vast majority of cases, the abductee remembers seeing only nostrils nearly flush against the smooth face.

In a very few cases, the entities are said to have pointed ears, but most witnesses report the absence of noticeable ears on the large, round heads.

A loose consensus of UFO researchers maintains that the strangers in our skies are reptilian or amphibian humanoids. Those who believe these beings are extraterrestrial aliens suspect that they have been interacting with our planet's evolution as explorers, genetic engineers, or merely observers.

Characteristics of UFO Abductees

Dr. R. Leo Sprinkle, an accomplished hypnotist and internationally known authority on UFO abductees, recently retired as director of counseling services at the University of Wyoming in Laramie, but he continues his extensive work with those who have had UFO encounters. Dr. Sprinkle has expressed his opinion that there may be hundreds of thousands of people who have met such beings as those described above, and whose memory of the experience may be repressed. Below he lists several characteristics common among UFO abductees:

1. *An episode of missing time.* Under hypnosis many people remember driving down the road and then being back in their car,   dazed, as if awakening from sleep. They know that something happened

between the two points of consciousness, but they can't fill in the missing time.

2. *Disturbing dreams.* The abductee will dream about flying saucers, about being pursued and captured, and being examined by doctors in white coats.

3. *Daytime flashbacks of UFO experiences.* While engaged in their normal daytime activities, abductees will flash back to some kind of UFO image or UFO entity.

4. *Strange compulsions.* Dr. Sprinkle tells of one man who for seven years felt compelled to dig a well at a particular spot. Under hypnosis, he revealed that a UFO being had told him that they would contact him again if he dug a well. And, of course, we all recall the compulsion of Richard Dreyfuss' character in *Close Encounters of the Third Kind* to sculpt Devil's Tower out of his mashed potatoes.

5. *A sudden interest in UFOs.* The abductee may suddenly give evidence of a compulsion to read about UFOs, ancient history, pyramids, or crystals without knowing why.

A Consistent Factor: Beings Wield Incredible Powers

Those who are abducted and believe themselves to have been actually transported to some alien craft or environment report a variety of experiences, everything from being probed to being sexually assaulted.

The one common experience shared by these abductees is the impression that these creatures wield incredible powers. Nearly all people who have encountered what they believe to be aliens say that the beings could appear or disappear at will and that they were able to make things move or respond to them with an unseen power. Moreover, these abductees say that it was impossible to resist an alien. These beings could do whatever they pleased to a person.

The Horror of Being Controlled by Aliens

It is that feeling of helplessness abductees find so frightening. To be suddenly paralyzed and taken away to be subjected to a bizarre medical examination against their will seemingly reduces them to the level of laboratory rats and robs them of a personal choice and free will. As one abductee commented, many individuals who have undergone the experience have completely revised their concept of the universe. Not only do other life forms exist but they also appear to be superior and in control.

Whitley Strieber, author of the best-selling book *Communion,* attempted to deal with his tension and anxiety over having undergone an abduction experience by writing about the encounter. He has admitted that when he first realized what had happened to him, he had even felt suicidal.

Strieber observed in *UFO* magazine in 1987 that "whatever is happening or whoever is here is here to stay and is here to stay for every one of us." He went on to state that many abductees with whom he had communicated had experienced a progression of emotions, moving from uneasy, fragmented recollection to a clear memory accompanied by fear. "We need to start learning to get beyond the fear to the stage of insight that comes from the emotional state of coping. Beyond that, the ultimate stage, which probably no one on Earth has reached yet, would be true understanding."

In his fifth book about the UFO enigma, *Confirmation: The Hard Evidence of Aliens Among Us*, Strieber states that the continuing abductions remain the work of the "Visitors," but as convinced as he is of their existence, he suggests that they may not be extraterrestrial in origin. "The visitors may be at once tempting us with their theater in the sky and forcing us into action by the outrageous invasion of our bodies represented by a close encounter," he writes.

For Many Abductees, the Terror Begins in Childhood

To present only one of hundreds of Dr. R. Leo Sprinkle's case histories, we recall the story of a woman named Barbara who, after undergoing hypnosis sessions with Dr. Sprinkle, learned that she had been a four-time victim of the UFO abductors.

Barbara had come to Dr. Sprinkle after she awakened feeling dizzy and nauseated and spotted with strange bruises on her body. She had a vague memory of someone holding her down and examining her mouth.

Under hypnosis, she remembered having been escorted to a small room with bright lights and being made to lie down on a soft couch. She seemed to be surrounded by small, hairless "children" with large black eyes and no ears. When the little children took her to another room, she became frightened and recalled feeling a sharp pain in her back.

Through subsequent sessions, Dr. Sprinkle learned that Barbara had first been abducted when she was only eight years old.

During what was determined to be her third encounter, she remembered being awakened by outside noises, which frightened her. Her next memory is of smallish beings taking her to a derby-shaped craft with flashing lights. This time she recalled being dealt sharp pains in her leg and head. She awakened later in her own bedroom with strange, unexplained bruises and other marks on her body.

During her fourth abduction, when she was about thirty-one, the hypnosis session revealed that she had been "floated" to her home to a spacecraft where she was given additional tests by alien beings and injected with some kind of fluid.

The Mystery of Alien Implants

Many people have told of aliens abducting them or injecting some substance into their bodies. Among those investigators trying their best to verify such accounts are Dr. Roger K. Leir, a podiatric surgeon, and hypnotherapist Derrel Sims.

Sims and Dr. Leir have reported on the series of surgeries conducted in August, 1995, during which three "highly anomalous implants" were removed from a man and woman who had both experienced what they were convinced had been alien abduction events. Two anomalous objects were removed from the woman's toes and a third was taken from the back of the man's hand.

Dr. Leir stated that the membranes on the objects were later analyzed as being composed of "a tough matrix of proteins from skin and blood. This would certainly explain why the body accepted the objects so readily." Metallurgists identified the "T" shaped metal object found in the big toe of the woman as being of "meteor-like" composition "...yet different...lacking nickel (or having only a trace in the third piece examined)."

Dr. Leir has remarked that in thirty years of medicine—and as former chief of the foot clinic at what is now called Cedars-Sinai Medical Center—he has removed "every sort of thing out of people's feet," but nothing like these objects.

One of the aspects of the devices that Dr. Leir found most amazing was the manner in which they were hidden in the bodies of the abductees without any visible scars were they had been implanted. Experts in other fields of expertise told him that if one were to stick the objects under an electron microscope, one would not be able to detect a simple microchip or any printed circuits.

"These devices are beyond that," he said. "They appear to be a unique combination of biological and electronic elements bonded together in a way we don't yet understand."

A Mysterious Metal Object

Harvard psychiatrist Dr. John Mack told Art of an abductee who had a small wire-like object that had worked its way down from high in a nasal sinus cavity into her throat. Neither a pathologist nor a radiologist was able to identify the object.

Upon examination by electron microscopy in October 1996, the specimen appeared to be an organic, plastic-like, three-lobed fiber with an internal structure organized into intricate layers   in a seemingly irregular manner. Its identity, function, and purpose remained unknown.

Some Abductees Have Insight into Their Experiences

An abductee referred to here as "Charles" said that he is haunted by the memory of lying on a table in a small metal-like room in some kind of vehicle. He is convinced that his experience was not a vision or a dream, and that he has insight into its meaning. What is significant about his experience is that something was implanted in his brain and he feels as though he is undergoing some "integration process."

Charles goes on to describe blackouts, spells of amnesia, and the urgent aching that he experiences inside. He believes that he is being prepared for some future event that he cannot fully understand.

Uncertain when his initial abduction occurred, Charles speculates that it may have been one night when he was driving home late from work. But he recalls seeing not more than ten feet above him a circular vehicle with a square bottom and a distended portion covered with white lights.

He remembers feeling groggy and light-headed as he stared at the object, then a beam of energy seemed to shoot through his entire body. "Something exploded in my brain and in my chest," he recalled. "I felt afraid, but I also felt that I could trust whatever experience was about to happen. Then I must have gone into a deep sleep."

But in spite of the deep altered state of consciousness, certain impressions come back to haunt him. He continues to recall images of smallish entities working around him in that circular craft.

Charles is growing more convinced that seeing UFOs or aliens is no longer necessary for the complete evolution of his thoughts and his awareness. He sees his physical experience with the aliens as a crude level of blending and communicating. He feels that the actual process of communion is on a much more subtle level:

> I know the beings deep inside. I feel them. I sense them. The old patterns of "show me, then I'll believe," have disappeared. I now feel the need to broaden and to sharpen my deeper levels of perception.

Abductors from Other Worlds or Other Dimensions?

Not only is there a growing acceptance among some researchers of the reality of abduction experiences, but a number of investigators are beginning to theorize that these "aliens" are not necessarily from some other planet or universe. Contrary to the traditionally held belief that these entities are extraterrestrial in origin, many researchers are starting to wonder if these creatures might not be from another dimension—or even if they are spiritual beings.

Whitley Strieber describes the power that these beings possess in his book, *Communion*, and he also indicates a sense that these aliens might even be demonic. But apart from the concept of a spiritual warfare between "good" aliens and "bad" aliens, what could these UFO abductors want? There seems no clear motive.

Perhaps it could be as simple as other life forms seeking to study and experiment with humans. On the other hand, it could really be a desire to take the souls of humans. Perhaps these so-called alien abductors are demons who have the commission to identify those humans whose minds and spirits may be controlled.

Exorcising the Alien Abductors

Recently, a number of avowed Christian UFO researchers have been advising those men and women being approached by such entities as the Grays as potential abductees to call out the name of Jesus Christ and "exorcise" them. In response, some near-abductees have testified that they tried it—and it worked. The abductors retreated upon hearing the name of Jesus being used to drive them away.

While it seems unlikely that actual physical beings from an extraterrestrial world would be thwarted from their goals by invoking the name of Jesus, such tactics just might work with the fallen angels.

It is interesting to note that many people who claim contact with aliens have been involved in the occult. And it is not uncommon for those who engage in certain occult practices to attempt to initiate contact with spirit beings. In fact, some occultists have reported contact with spirit entities who have similar traits as those described by those abductees who have encountered what they believe to be aliens.

If these beings should be from the same source, this should not really come as a surprise. Given that there are many more people than ever before engaged in occult practices because of the New Age spiritual movement, this may well explain the increase in reported "alien" experiences over the last thirty years.

UFOs Achieve Cult Followings

There is no question that some people have made a religion out of the UFO contact experience and there are many individuals who have achieved both local and international attention by claiming to "channel" messages from alien Space Brothers and Sisters.

The Heaven's Gate disciples focused worldwide negative attention on such UFO cults when they conducted a mass suicide at Rancho Santa Fe on March 26, 1997. Others, who rally around a particular channeler relaying cosmic guidance, benignly serve the life force, rather than death. Some even gather together in their own communities, such as the one in Brazil, just fifty miles from Brasilia, the nation's capital. Called the Valley of the Dawn, all 5,000 citizens of this community are members of a UFO religion founded by a former truck driver named Aunt Neiva.

Are Abductees Recalling Actual Physical Experiences?

While some make a religion out of contactee and abductee experiences, others are beginning to have serious doubts about this facet of the great UFO mystery. Writing in a recent issue of *Alternate Perceptions*, Dr. Greg Little takes a hard line with "a number of prominent UFO speakers, 'researchers,' abductees, and a mass of paranoia-prone people" who, he says, are driven to fake cases and documents, embellish reports, lie about being abducted, and spread rumors. Dr. Little charges:

> It's time that the ufologists who are genuine in their interest in solving the mystery accept that 95% of abduction claims are spurious—just as 95% of UFO reports are. At least nine out of every

10 "abductees" I have interviewed are not telling a genuine abduction report.

Even Betty Hill, perhaps the most famous abductee of all, is not happy with the current crop of those who claim experiences similar to the one she underwent with her husband Barney on September 19, 1961. In her 1995 book, *A Common Sense Approach to UFOs*, she is especially tough on the manner in which certain irresponsible UFO researchers with little formal training in hypnosis create flights of fantasy in the minds of alleged abductees, then label the result as genuine accounts of alien abductions.

Long-time UFO researcher and author Timothy Green Beckley expressed similar concerns:

> I guess I worry about some of the UFO researchers who hypnotize people who believe they were abducted. Not only do the abductees feed back pretty much what the researcher already believes, but I cannot help thinking that it could be dangerous to be hypnotized by someone without any real background in medicine, psychology, or counseling. Some of these abductees are allowed to "remember" some pretty horrible and frightening things, and I worry that some less stable subjects could be emotionally scarred by their hypnosis sessions.

As a long-time student of the paranormal, as well as ufology, I cannot help recognizing some old familiar demons of the human psyche emerging in contemporary clothing. The incubus and succubus phenomena of the Middle Ages—with its emphasis on sexual molestation and the crossbreeding of humans and demons—doesn't seem too far off from the UFO abductors of today. And when abductees talk about implants and peculiar markings on their bodies, I think of phenomena such as stigmata and the power of suggestion, which can cause bloody wounds to open or close on fanatical or hysterical subjects.

Abductions Caused by Mechanical/Technical Process?

John Thompson, former MUFON Georgia State Director, has theorized that no physical abductions occur, but such illusions are caused by a

mental/technical process we can't comprehend. The aliens' real goal is to influence mankind's thinking process...[an alien intelligence] keeps revisiting people to "condition" and "recondition" them as they see fit. In other words, what "abductions" are about is mind control...to keep humans from trying to stop whatever the earthbound aliens are doing.

Their ultimate goal may be for man to create a climate right for one-world rule, with the aliens as the ultimate unseen rulers. The plan is to ensure mankind's enslavement or destruction (as Dr. David Jacobs correctly implies, but incorrectly understands). I don't think [abductions have] anything to do with making hybrids and breeding. That's all smoke, much of it created by the alleged "abductees" themselves. The goal is...the control of mankind. [Excerpts from George Filer's Files, June 7, 1998]

Aliens, Monsters, Demons, and Angels on Demand

Neuroscientist Michael Persinger maintains that he has created such a "mental/technical" device that can simulate the experiences reported by abductees. Those volunteers who enter Persinger's chamber in his laboratory at Laurentian University in Sudbury, Ontario, don a snug-fitting modified motorcycle helmet equipped on both sides with coiled wire cylinders. The magnetic fields that he will send to the brain via computer will induce perceptions of aliens, angels, demons, or other monsters of the human mind.

Persinger contends that the brain is highly sensitive to information produced by complex or irregularly pulsed magnetic fields. Some regions deep within such temporal lobes are strongly associated with the regulation of emotions and are highly unstable electrically. If those areas are stimulated, people may be induced to report mystical encounters and the appearance of strange beings.

Persinger charges that science has done very little to study the impact of electromagnetic fields on consciousness and behavior. Few studies have examined how the ordinary states of human imagery and awareness might be affected by the increasingly complex electromagnetic corridors that contemporary humans inhabit. And, then, of course, certain individuals may be more vulnerable to such electromagnetic influences because their temporal lobes may be more electrically unstable.

The Continuing Horror of Animal Mutilations

Controversy also manifests strongly in nearly every aspect of the phenomenon of alleged animal mutilations being conducted by alien scientists for a variety of purposes. Primary of which, according to one oft-cited reason is the alleged deal that a branch of the secret government cut with the aliens to enable them to sustain themselves on Earth by ingesting a particular enzyme, or hormonal secretion, most readily obtained from the tongues and throats of cattle.

The most prominent and respected researcher in the bizarre field of animal mutilations is Linda Moulton Howe, author of *Glimpses of Other Realities*. Howe has documented hundreds of abnormal, inexplicable deaths of animals, mostly cattle and horses on the open range. These animals died because of bloodless excisions and the removal of eyes, organs, and genitals.

According to forensic pathologists who examined many of these animals, traditional surgical instruments were not used, but the incisions were perhaps the result of an advanced laser technology. Further, it appears no coincidence that this same type of animal mutilation occurs worldwide with the same kinds of animals every time.

Regardless of your skepticism toward the subject of cattle mutilations, it does comprise a genuine mystery. Every time that a critter winds up dead with its tongue, eyes, ears, anus, udder, and genitalia removed without apparently shedding a drop of blood and without the anonymous surgeons leaving any tracks whatsoever, the usual suspects—aliens, satanic cultists, and unmarked black helicopters—are sought for questioning. But thus far no culprit has ever been apprehended.

As Howe has asked, "How can you remove an entire nine-inch long heart from the inside of a cow without making an incision on the outside of the body?"

Interestingly, veterinarians and forensic scientists who have investigated the mysterious mutilations usually describe the blood as appearing to have been drained with no resultant vascular collapse. The known technology that could process such an accomplishment does not exist, and if it did, it would seem to have to be pretty big and heavy to manipulate animals weighing well over 1500 pounds or more.

When she began her intensive research in the fall of 1979, Howe suspected that there was some sort of contamination in the environment and that our government, in cooperation with other governments, was secretly harvesting tissue and fluids for examination. But she could not fathom why government agencies working in secrecy would be so careless as to leave the carcasses of the animals, creating alarm and anger.

Her first conversations were with ranchers and law enforcement officers, who reluctantly informed her of the sightings of glowing disks in the vicinity of the cattle mutilations. Some people even told her of having seen non-human entities at the scene.

Most investigators have eliminated the possibility that predators or scavengers could so neatly incise and remove select organs from their victims. And the obvious problem with blaming predators and scavengers was the fact that all the rest of the animal remained intact. Why wouldn't the classic one/two attack of the killing predator and the clean-up team of scavengers have left nothing but bones and a few tufts of hair? Some researchers even reported seeing dead vultures, buzzards, hawks, and other birds lying dead nearby, as if they had been somehow killed in their normal dining procedures of picking the bones clean.

Tracks or markings of a conventional nature—tire imprints, human or animal tracks—have never been found near a mutilated carcass, but some farmers and ranchers have reported the indentations of a tripod or a crop circle nearby. And there have been those eerie reports of UFOs seen in the area and in the immediate vicinity of a cattle mutilation.

More Clues to the Mutilation Mystery

Linda Howe has discussed her meeting with a former Army Signal Corps instructor—who also worked for the CIA between 1957 and 1960. The Army instructor told her that he had read highly classified reports concerning extraterrestrial aliens and animal mutilations at that time. The first worldwide report of an animal mutilation was that of the famous horse "Snippy" in September 1967. Therefore, to learn that there were government reports on the subject many years prior to that date seems to reinforce a lot of nasty rumors about secret government agencies and extraterrestrials.

Brad received a number of letters in and around the year 1967 that came from summer vacationers who had come upon grisly circles of mutilated animals. In one instance, twenty or so rabbits, and in another, a dozen or so moose.

Howe now states that she has accumulated certain newspaper clippings that go back as far as 1961 in Alabama. Her current source's files go back even earlier to the late 1940s.

The Debunkers Have Their Say

In May 1979, Kenneth Rommel, an FBI agent with twenty-eight years of experience, specializing in counter-intelligence, was made director of "Operation Animal Mutilation," under the aegis of the district attorney's office of New Mexico's First Judicial District, funded by a grant from the U.S. Justice Department's Law Enforcement Assistance Administration. Rommel enlisted the aid of veterinarians, livestock association officials, forensic pathologists, chemists, and a host of county, state, and federal officers and agents.

His conclusion, after personally inspecting twenty-five carcasses of mutilated cattle and spending roughly a year assimilating all the knowledge of his army of experts, was that good old Mother Nature had simply been fulfilling one of her primary responsibilities, that of keeping the countryside clean.

One by one, he said, he had eliminated UFOs, environmental testing, biological experiments, Satanists, and all the other possible culprits off his list of suspects. The real perpetrators of the mystery of animal mutilations were predators and scavengers. All the tales of bloodless carcasses, organs removed with surgical precision, and so forth, were the work of creative journalists, excitable ranchers, paranoid UFO conspiracy theorists, and rumor mongers.

After 17 years of gathering dust in the archives, Jack Hitt revived Kenneth Rommel's investigations of cattle mutilations for his article, "Operation Moo," for the February 1997 issue of *Gentleman's Quarterly.* Agreeing with Rommel's basic conclusions, Hitt added his theory that the cattle died of such mundane causes as eating poisonous plants. Then, after the body had lain on the lonely prairie and ripened for a few days, the soft tissues of various organs would be easy pecking for birds and other scavengers. The very suggestion of alien surgeons was soundly pooh-poohed.

The Truth Is Still Hidden

Can such a large number of ranchers, farmers, veterinarians, forensic scientists, and UFO investigators, who perceive the mystery of cattle mutilations so very differently from Kenneth Rommel's official report be so very wrong and mistaken about what they observed?

We believe that we have not yet heard the final word regarding the sinister mystery of cattle mutilations.

And the controversy over alien abductions of humans has only begun to define itself along clear battle lines. On the one hand, extraterrestrial or multidimensional beings kidnap men, women, and children for undeclared medical experiments or for purposes of systematic crossbreeding. On the other, illusions perpetrated by the "black magic" of mental/technical machinery designed to foster images of pseudo-physical abductions for the express purpose of mind control and the enslavement of our species.

Neither have we heard the final word regarding the frightening enigma of alien abductions.

SEVEN

ANGELS VERSUS DEMONS —
OR GOOD ALIENS VERSUS BAD ALIENS?

A number of recent polls reveal that people are seeing angels on a regular basis—and they're not just talking about those three attractive and compassionate beings that the hallowed halls of CBS television offers them every Sunday night in the form of Monica, Tess, and Andrew. According to their own testimony, thousands of men and women are truly being touched by real heavenly angels in times of illness, stress, and personal crises.

On December 27, 1993, *Time* magazine presented the results of their survey which stated that 69% of Americans believe in the existence of angels—and 46% believe that they have their own guardian angel watching over them. Of those individuals polled by the newsmagazine, 32% affirm that they have personally felt the presence of angels in their lives.

Guides, Guardians and Supernatural Companions

Brad once nearly punched an angel in the face. The hooded spirit teacher who appeared in his bedroom one evening in 1972 appeared so solid and so three-dimensional that he judged him to be an intruder. However, the blow never landed. Brad remembers that he felt:

> all of my strength draining from my body. I felt like a balloon that had suddenly lost all of its air. I had never felt so weak and so help-less in my life. I collapsed in a heap and be-gan to cry in fear and confusion.

The entity obviously took no offense at Brad's all too-human reaction. It told him not to be afraid, then, placing him in an altered-state-of-consciousness, dic-tated concepts that later became one of his most popular and respected works, *Revelation: The Divine Fire.*

The spirit teacher has returned on four other occa-sions. Three times it rendered valuable advice, and once it prescribed a certain combination of nutrients when Brad was mired in a painful medical crisis.

Identifying the Personal Spiritual Companion or Guide

Since 1968, Brad has been distributing various questionnaires to readers of his books and to those who have attended his lectures and the seminars that he has presented with his wife, Sherry. Well over 20,000 men and women have returned the questionnaire dealing with the individual mystical experience and a very high percentage of those individuals are convinced that they have experienced an encounter with angels, guides, various supernatural companions, and extra-terrestrial or multidimensional beings.

- 38% of those who responded to the questionnaire state that they have witnessed the physical presence of an angel.

- 34% are convinced that they had an encounter with an alien being of an extraterrestrial or multidimensional nature.

- 50% believe that they have a personal spirit guide or guardian angel, whether or not they have seen a physical manifestation of the guide.

- 37% state that they have seen the form of entity that they can identify only as a Light Being.

- 35% have interpreted the manifestation that they have witnessed as that of a Holy Figure, such as Mother Mary, Moses, Jesus, and so forth.

People Are Being Touched by Demons & Angels

During this same remarkable time period in which we dwell, a number of heinous crimes have been committed that truly seem to be the work of men, women, and children possessed by demonic forces.

In 1997 numerous terrible murders by school children took place across the United States. In the same year, a teenager in Japan claimed that an evil spirit took control of him and forced him to bludgeon to death a primary school girl and to kill and decapitate an eleven-year-old retarded boy. Apparently, the spirit also told him to keep the head in his room for several days so it might speak to him. Those who knew the youthful assassin said that he had an obsession with horror movies, the occult, and the lives of serial killers.

In January 1998, a 17 year-old Sayville, New York high school senior—an All-American cheerleader type— was killed by her mother and an older sister who believed that she was possessed by demons.

Sixty Percent of Americans Believe in the Devil

It is such incomprehensible crimes as the above that prompted 60% of Americans to declare in a recent poll that they believe in the Devil. Three decades ago, in 1964, only 37% of Americans would admit that they believed in Satan. Almost as many Canadians, 50%, state their belief that there is an evil force that stalks the Earth. In Europe, the percentages are lower: France, 17%; Great Britain, 21%; Germany, 25%.

Jeffrey Victor, author of *Satanic Panic: The Creation of a Contemporary Legend*, says that Americans are becoming more convinced of the reality of Satan due to the increasing number of major problems facing the country today.

> Families are under great pressure due to declining incomes and the social pressures of drugs, youth crime and gangs, increasing teen sex and so on. People who have been in stable jobs for twenty years are being let go because of increasing technology.

Victor goes on to state that men and women are searching for reasons why their lives have gone so terribly wrong in recent years:

> The United States has a tradition of bedrock religious belief, so it's not surprising that rapidly increasing numbers of people are convinced in the existence of the Devil.

And while there may be rapidly increasing numbers of people just coming to believe in Satan, there are perhaps many more who have believed in his hellish majesty all along.

A Spiritual War Is Taking Place All Around Us

Father Malachi Martin, a Jesuit scholar and a leading authority on demons and exorcism, has often and firmly stated his conviction there is a spiritual war being conducted today: "And as St. Paul said, it's a war with the spirits. It's a war with the forces of evil, the invisible forces that want men's souls."

Father Martin refers here to Ephesians 6:12: "For we wrestle not against flesh and blood, but against principalities, against powers, against the rulers of the darkness of this world, against spiritual hosts of wickedness in high places." [King James Version] Interestingly, George M. Lamsa's translation from the Aramaic, is even more pointed: "For your conflict is not only with flesh and blood, but also with the angels, and with powers, with the rulers of this world of darkness, and with the evil spirits under the heavens."

There is no question in Father Martin's mind that demons—the fallen angels—do attack and possess hu-

man beings "in their will and intellect." And the great
spiritual warfare is over human beings.

According to Father Martin, a former member of the
Vatican intelligence network:

> Well over 50% of persons suffering psychiatric
> problems are really possessed by demons. Many
> multiple personality disorders have been shown
> to be cases of demonic possession. A person
> may be possessed by more than one demon, and
> one demon may possess several people at one
> time.

> In some instances, the same demon may inhabit
> the members of a family for generations. Such
> possession is consensual, and the demon is ac-
> tually "nourished" by those entities he possesses.
> You can't be possessed without knowing it or
> against your will. You needn't be afraid that
> you're possessed and don't know it. That doesn't
> happen.

But how would a person know if he or she were possessed? Father Martin explains:

> If in your life there is some imperative coming out
> of left field, not of your choice, but commanding
> you, urging you to do something, to yield, to be
> controlled, that can herald demonic activity.

He also warns against undisciplined channeling,
careless meditative practices, and playing around with
such devices as the Ouija board.

Entities from Other Worlds Have Always Been With Us

Throughout the course of our history there have always been accounts of humanlike beings, some with alleged supernatural powers, who have been called Angels, Elves, Devas, Star People, Light Beings, Space Brothers, Grays—and, on occasion, demons and devils.

These entities have been seen traveling about in fiery chariots, mysterious globes of light, strange aerial vehicles, or blinding flashes of light. Sometimes they reveal themselves as benevolent entities, arriving mysteriously to give advice or to grant a miracle. On other occasions, they have been accused of abducting adults, kidnapping children, even murdering those who trusted them too much.

The place of origin for these beings has been identified as heaven, hell, the Earth's interior, other worlds, other galaxies, other dimensions. And while these beings are proclaimed to be very different from us, there seems always to be something very familiar about them that provokes vague stirrings in the deeper levels of the human psyche.

And now, in 1999, the fact that the presence of these entities seems to be increasing as we near the millennium, numerous evangelical Christians and other fundamentalists are growing concerned that they might well be the supernatural warriors of the Apocalypse.

It's Easy to Confuse Aliens with Angels

Some researchers assert that entities from UFOs are serving as spiritual guides for the men and women of Earth. The more conventionally religious theorize that we are confusing heavenly angelic guardians as alien beings because our advanced technology and our contemporary culture find extraterrestrial entities easier to accept than messengers sent from God.

In both the Old and the New Testaments we are told that angels are divided into two vast hosts: one, obedient to God and active in good ministries for humankind; the other, intent on annoying and harming humans and bringing about their enslavement. Certain UFO researchers have suggested a similar division of purpose and motive for the aliens. And surely, it cannot be denied that both aliens and angels are extraterrestrials.

As used in scripture, the term "angel" indicates an office, rather than a person. An angel is simply a messenger, one who is sent to accomplish whatever mission has been assigned to him or her by God.

Although angels are frequently called spirits, it is often implied in the Bible that they do possess corporeal bodies, but dwell on a higher plane of existence than humans. When seen on Earth, angels have always appeared youthful, physically attractive, commanding. They are, in fact, described in much the same manner as UFO contactees have described their "Space Brothers and Sisters."

Do the Contactees Listen to Angels or Aliens?

Since the 1950s, UFO researchers have listened to men and women who claim contact with aliens. Many of these contactees insist that the entities told them that they had been "seeded" here on Earth and that the aliens had a serious interest in their welfare.

Whether this be some dramatic attempt at monitoring a hybrid species of Earthlings or whether such statements are the products of men and women undergoing some kind of mystical experience, the fact remains that thousands of contactees have declared a special relationship between themselves and otherworldly beings. Dozens of men and women have claimed close encounters with extraterrestrial beings and supernatural entities, and many of these stories are quite compelling.

In his *Catchers of Heaven*, Dr. Michael Wolf documents his lifelong friendship with Kolta, an entity commonly referred to as a "Gray" in contemporary ufology. While Grays generally have a sinister reputation, Dr. Wolf insists that his cosmic friend has consistently demonstrated warmth, affection, spirituality, and cosmic love in their decades' long interaction.

Santa Barbara psychotherapist Donna Higbee has said that attitudes appear to be changing among abductees who formerly spoke only of having been traumatized, physically abused, and violated. "Now they are saying that their abductors have only spiritual and/or benevolent motives behind their actions."

Even Whitley Strieber, whose *Communion* shocked many men and women into remembering similar experiences of abduction, has begun referring to himself as a contactee, rather than an abductee.

UFO researcher Preston Dennet has detailed numerous cases of human/alien interaction during which extraterrestrial or multidimensional beings have cured earthlings of everything from cancer to the common cold.

Lyssa Royal is among those who believe that the aliens are helping humankind to reach levels of higher awareness. In her *Visitors from Within*, she sets forth the notion that when humans undergo alien contacts that they consider horrifying, they are often dredging up negative aspects of their own inner-selves. When we truly discover who we are, Ms. Royal predicts, we will discover who they are.

James Gilliland, author of *Becoming Gods: A Reunion with the Source*, also believes that the Grays and other extraterrestrial beings are generally about the task of raising human consciousness and he says that he knows their true identity. They are highly evolved entities from Andromeda, who have in the past been mythologized as Archangels. As Gilliland explains:

> They are the overseers. They understand why the changes are necessary; they know that you are eternal, and this is part of your evolution as well as the planet's need to rejuvenate herself.

The Dangers, Hazards, and Challenges of Becoming a UFO Contactee

Those UFO contactees who are convinced that they are in direct communication with extraterrestrial or multidimensional intelligences very often claim a personal and physical contact with the being that originated the contact experience. Once the initial contact has been made with the contactee, the method of receiving messages is usually through channeling and/or mental telepathy. Along with a heightening of apparent extrasensory abilities, the contactee is very often left with a timetable of dramatic predictions of future events.

In spite of such setbacks as occasional unfulfilled prophecies, a good number of the space intelligences' channelers continued to be imbued with an almost religious fervor to spread the messages that have been entrusted to them.

Over many years of investigation by various UFO re-searchers, the philosophical and metaphysical content of the essential messages given to the contactees is nearly always the same. If we were to distill the com-mon Outer Space Apocrypha, we would present such familiar concepts as the following:

- Humans are not alone in the universe. Older, wiser entities from other worlds have now come to Earth to reach humans and to teach them to embrace the oneness of all living things in the universe.

- Humans have not been good caretakers of their planet. They have polluted the skies and the waters and endangered the natural balance of their earth.

- The Space Intelligences have advanced information that they wish to impart to the people of Earth. As earthlings mature, they will be invited to join an in-tergalactic spiritual federation.

- The Space Intelligences are here to teach, to awaken the human spirit, to help humankind rise to higher levels of vibration, so that they will be able to enter new dimensions. Humankind stands now in the transitional period of a New Age.

- If the inhabitants of Earth should fail to raise their vibratory rate within a set period of time, severe Earth changes and major cataclysms will rock the planet. Such disasters will not end the world, but will serve as vast crucibles to burn off the dross of unreceptive humanity.

Admittedly, there is nothing truly universe-shaking in such pronouncements. On their surface, the messages of the contactees seem filled with basic truths, real environmental concerns, and feel-good metaphysics, hardly the kind of meaty stuff one might expect from beings who have traveled from faraway worlds to impart their knowledge to us.

On the other hand, it could be that we are slowly being provided with the bits and pieces of some super cosmic jigsaw puzzle through the contactees, which one day, if properly assembled, will give us a more complete picture of the entire UFO mystery.

Defining the Process by Which UFO Contact Is Made

How does the UFO contactee, the Space Intelligences channeler, receive his or her initial contact?

Throughout over forty years of researching the UFO contactee, a somewhat definite pattern has emerged.

- The contactees, when they were driving or walking in lonely places saw a UFO on the ground or hovering low overhead and heard a slight humming sound emanating from the vehicle. A warm ray of "light" emanated from the UFO and touched the contactee on the neck, the crown of the head, or the middle of the forehead. In certain instances, the contactees may lose consciousness at this point, and upon awakening discover that they cannot account for a period of time amounting to several minutes or several hours.

- In other cases, the contactees may have been sitting alone in their room, quietly deep in thought, perhaps meditating, even sleeping, when they are brought back to full consciousness by the mysterious appearance of a being. Very often, the "missing time" phenomenon is noted upon a more complete recollection of the visitation.

- The contactees who remain conscious and retain a clear memory of the experience say that an attractive Space Intelligence, a Gray, or a "voice" inside their head tells them that they have been selected for a particular mission because they are, in reality, someone very special. Those who lapsed into unconsciousness during the contact experience soon receive an identical message concerning their special status among humans through "channeling."

- Many contactees are told that they are reincarnations of noble individuals from Earth's past. A good number are informed that they are really hybrid beings who were planted on Earth as very small children. Or, in an alternate story, they have the consciousness of Space Intelligences that was placed within them before birth.

- Many contactees recall that they were given a vial of liquid and asked to drink it. The Space Intelligences remind them that they have drunk of the elixir before—either as children in their present life experience or as cosmonauts in a prior existence.

- In any event, the contactees are made to feel that they are very special human beings who have been carefully selected to bring about a special mission of the Space Intelligences. Thus, as will surely be noted, one of the greatest personal obstacles for the contactees to overcome is unbridled ego.

• Nearly all contactees have suffered through several days and nights of restlessness, irritability, sleeplessness, and unusual dreams immediately after the initial contact experience.

• After a period of a week to several months, the contactee feels prepared to go forth and preach the cosmic gospel.

• Very few of the contactees feel any fear toward the Space Intelligences. Most of them claim to look forward to a promised return visit from the beings.

• Families and friends report that the contactee is a changed person after the encounter with the Space Intelligence.

• Contactees very often become so committed to the Outer Space Gospel that they seem unconcerned about their personal welfare or the needs of their families.

For the Bible Tells Us So

For many years now, certain ufologists have suggested that the Judeo-Christian Bible is the greatest record of UFO contacts ever assembled. Without wishing to offend the religious beliefs of any traditional religionists, it is true that scripture is filled with accounts of glowing aerial vehicles, angels walking among humankind, and certain humans receiving prophetic messages. And it does appear that a similar kind of contact and communication exists today between the UFO entities and an ever-growing number of humans.

In his provocative *The Bible and Flying Saucers*, published in 1968, Rev. Barry Downing, a respected Protestant minister, argues that some of the biblical passages regarding angels may best be understood in the light of contemporary UFO research. Other researchers, such as G. C. Schellhorn, have continued to explore evidence of flying saucers in the Bible and the holy books of other major religions.

If the Bible and other holy works really do contain a number of UFO contact stories, then perhaps the predicted final battle between the Forces of Light and Darkness (Armageddon) may also address itself directly to our times. For while many UFO contactees believe their interaction with "Space Brothers and Sisters" to be totally benevolent, it cannot be denied that some of the space beings have deceived and embarrassed their human channels.

And then there is the uncomfortable matter of certain UFO abductions and other hostile activities that would appear at the very least to suggest disrespect for humankind.

In an article for the *MUFON UFO Journal* (May 1990), Rev. Barry Downing theorized that the Grays may really be benevolent, superior beings, who disguise themselves so that we may not readily perceive their "vastly superior reality."

In a later article in the same journal (February 1992), John White agreed that certain Grays may be good, "just as there are good and bad people," but he argued that if there were any angels conducting the abductions of human beings, then they were fallen angels or demonic entities.

Fallen Angels May Attack Us from Our Inner Space

According to Persian and Chaldean tradition, the Ahrimanes are the fallen angels, who out of revenge for being expelled from heaven, continually torment the apex of God's creation, the human inhabitants of Earth. The old legends have it that the Ahrimanes finally decided to inhabit the space between the Earth and the fixed stars, which is called Ahrimane-Abad.

Military and aviation historian Trevor James Constable has come to the conclusion that it is the Ahrimanic powers that are trying to seize control of our planet. He believes that Inner Space, not Outer Space, is the invasion route chosen by the Ahrimanic powers.

Constable is not alone in suggesting that the UFO beings may be ethereal, rather than, physical entities. And his concerns echo those of Father Malachi Martin that the goal of the struggle in this great spiritual warfare is for the souls of humans, rather than their planet.

"Man is at once the goal of the battle and the battleground," Constable states emphatically. The UFO entities have devised contact encounters with ingenuous humans and set about deceiving them to believe that material craft and beings from an extraterrestrial source are invading Earth. But always, their ultimate goal is to enslave the very soul, mind, and destiny of humankind.

Some contactees insist that a mass invasion of Earth would already have taken place if it had not been for the intervention of other, more benevolent interplanetary beings. A kind of "Interplanetary Council" is doing what it can to halt the invasion of our planet and to correct the vast number of wrongs that have already been dealt to the human species.

Perhaps *Both* Angels and Aliens Have Many Faces

In UFO research, we are left with the argument that there appear to be those angels or aliens who are genuinely concerned about our welfare and our spiritual and physical evolution. Then there are those who, at best, seem largely indifferent to our personal needs and our species continued existence. On the other hand, we might somehow perceive different aspects of the same entities.

Dr. John Mack has commented how such cruel and traumatic experiences as abductions could also be considered spiritually illuminating:

> Sometimes our most useful spiritual learning and growth comes at the hands of rough teachers who have little respect for our conceits, psychological defenses, or established points of view.... The alien beings that abductees speak about seem to...come from another domain that is felt to be closer to the source of being or primary creation. They have been described...as intermediaries or emissaries from God, even as angels.... The acknowledgment of their existence, after the initial ontological shock, is sometimes...the first step in the opening of consciousness to a universe that is no longer simply material. Abductees come to appreciate that the universe is filled with a variety of intelligence and is itself intelligent. They develop a sense of awe before a mysterious cosmos that becomes sacred and "en-

souled." The sense of separation from all the rest of creation breaks down....

Can it be that we humans are engaged in some great teaching experience with some as yet undeclared cosmic tutors who are guiding us and directing us, but refusing to show us the answers until we have achieved our own realization of the Great Mystery?

EIGHT

SPACE ANOMALIES

Dr. Brian O'Leary, author of *Mars, 1999* and *Miracle in the Void,* worked with the late Dr. Carl Sagan at Cornell University and was an Apollo astronaut in the NASA space program. O'Leary believes that we can feasibly visit Mars by utilizing one of its moons, most likely Phobos, as a base for manned and unmanned probes. He speculates that it is very likely that water can be located in the soil of Phobos and that carbon compounds are present for restocking fuel and life support systems.

O'Leary said that he was supportive of the Mars Pathfinder probes, but he has been disappointed by NASA's lack of vision. He has been especially frustrated by their failure to adequately investigate the Cydonia region that supports the mile-wide structure that so resembles a human or humanoid face.

After 15 years of researching the Cydonia enigma, O'Leary has concluded that there exists an

...unwitting alliance between those who call themselves scientists, who are close-minded to this inquiry, and the powers that be, who are very clearly covering up this information.

Richard Hoagland Surveys the Monuments of Mars

Richard Hoagland, author of *The Monuments of Mars*, has studied and gathered what he calls scientific data on several provocative photos of the surface of Mars taken by NASA's Viking probe in 1976. These photos show certain formations that appear to be unusual compared to the rest of the geologic features on the Martian surface, and he contends that these formations are artificial, not unlike the pyramids or Sphinx of Egypt.

In fact, Hoagland goes so far as to say that these structures may have been constructed by some alien race thousands or even millions of years ago. He also notes the possibility is the same for Europa, a moon of Jupiter, as seen in Voyager mission photos.

Hoagland saw the mysterious sphinx-like face in the Martian landscape known as Cydonia (which is not to be confused with Sedona, the New Age Mecca in Arizona) for the first time in the summer of 1976:

NASA's Viking had taken 100,000 pictures of Mars. When we were shown the initial image of the "face," we were told that the spacecraft took another frame a few hours later and the whole image had gone away. It was all a trick of the lighting. And we believed them! Nobody even asked to see the second picture!

Hoagland was a consultant to NASA's Goddard Space Flight Center from 1975 to 1980. During the historic Apollo missions to the Moon, he served as science advisor to the CBS news department. In 1984 he organized the Independent Mars Investigation (renamed the Enterprise Mission), and fiercely advocated that NASA has been withholding knowledge concerning structures and artifacts discovered on Mars and the Moon that would yield proof of extraterrestrial civilizations. Hoagland believes that there are two space programs in existence: one to appease the taxpayers and another conducted by a top-secret group with a hidden agenda.

When the project scientist at NASA first revealed pictures of the face on Mars, Hoagland recalls that the man made a joke of the preposterous thought that it could really be an artificial structure. Everyone laughed with him because after all, everyone knew that NASA's highest objective was to find evidence that we are not alone in the universe.

The Secret Message of Cydonia

Hoagland's subsequent investigations have yielded what he believes to be evidence not only of the mysterious face, but also of several four and five-sided pyramids. In his educated opinion, no natural force could have fashioned such regularly repeated geometric structures.

Hoagland speculates that perhaps the Message of Cydonia is that a code has been laid out for those who are bright enough to figure it out, to determine the mathematics and the geometry that can open new gateways to the universe.

Pictures of a Martian "Sandbox"

Richard Hoagland was undaunted on April 7, 1998, when NASA's Mars Global Surveyor sent back photographs of the Face on Mars that were clearly expected to debunk any theories that an ancient Martian or other extraterrestrial civilization had carved the mysterious features. After 22 years of waiting for clearer photographs that would confirm the handiwork of intelligent life on Mars, the new pictures showed only eroded landscape and a pile of rocks. The close-ups resembled photos of a "sandbox."

Shrugging over the apparent reality that NASA had "erased" the face, Hoagland stated that he was really far more interested in the ruins of what has been called the City of Cydonia than with the sphinx-like structure. And now he can only wonder if the photographers at NASA missed obtaining better pictures of the city on purpose.

"This is ancient, ruined architecture we're seeing," he told the May 11, 1998 issue of USA TODAY. Hoagland says NASA has photographs confirming his theory but won't release them because they would so shock Earth that civilization might collapse. "They're seeing things they did not expect. That's why they're not showing all the data."

Cydonia Attracts the Attention of Dr. Van Flandern

However, some scientists heard Richard Hoagland's clarion call for more honest dispersal on the part of NASA. Geologists, photography experts, astronomers, and architects were beginning to analyze the Surveyor's photographs with renewed interest.

Astronomer Dr. Tom Van Flandern, former head of celestial mechanics at the U.S. Naval Observatory and current head of a Washington, D.C. group called Meta Research, doesn't believe that "UFO pilots" constructed the ruins on Mars. Neither does he accept NASA's easy dismissal of the "ruins." In fact because the Martian region photographed as so many odd patterns and shapes, Dr. Van Flandern places the odds at a billion to one that all of them could have occurred naturally:

> That the surrounding desert is flat and feature-less is of great significance in contrast to this sudden 400-meter object rising at a regular height all around with perfectly straight sides. Ninety-degree angles are common; the bottom is symmetric. The sockets and foreheads are well defined, and even match up well with the original photo of the face.

Continuing with his analysis, Dr. Van Flandern stated:

> Before seeing this new image, we knew that a "fractal" content implied a natural origin, while regularity, angularity, and symmetry implied ar-tificiality. I see almost no fractality with the ex-ception of the nose bridge, the feature least pro-tected from wind erosion. I do see smooth lines and curves, right angles and corners (including one in the "furrowed" eyebrow) and lots of sym-metry, especially detailed symmetry in the head-dress enclosure. And that symmetry is not sim-ple symmetry, as when duplicating a profile, but full 3-D symmetry. For example, the enclosure

wraps all the way around with both its inner and outer boundaries, yet remains of uniform height and symmetric shape. Nowhere does the mesa overlap or get confounded with this boundary.

Dr. Van Flandern was completely impressed with the artificial construction on Mars:

In my considered opinion, there is no longer room for reasonable doubt of the artificial origin of the face mesa—and I've never concluded 'no room for reasonable doubt' about anything before in my thirty-five-year scientific career.

Researchers Insist that Alien Bases Exist on the Moon

Throughout the years, Richard Hoagland has not been the only theorist using NASA's own photographs, as well as the pictures taken by the Russian space program to make a provocative case that proof of extraterrestrial life exists on the Moon and on Mars. A large number of other theorists have also identified with the questions of mysterious space artifacts and anomalies.

In his *We Discovered Alien Bases on the Moon*, former NASA jet propulsion engineer Fred Steckling was among the first to sound the alert that we were not being told the full story concerning the astronauts' visit to our planet's satellite. David Hatcher Childress' *Extraterrestrial Archaeology* continued the quest for more complete revelations from our space program.

This was followed by Cynthia Turnage's, *Extraterrestrials Are on the Moon: The Photographic Evidence*, in which she accuses NASA's scientists of a wall of silence concerning the concrete evidence of extraterrestrial life that has been captured on film. Ms. Turnage further suggests that some other government agency outside of NASA may be pressuring its scientists to cover up any evidence of alien life.

Others, such as Peter Beter, claim that Russia is on the Moon and that they, rather than extraterrestrials, may have secretly been mining its resources for many years. From time to time, alleged Air Force veterans, insisting upon complete anonymity, swear that the United States established a secret base on the Moon in 1970 and that they discovered an alien base on its dark side.

Persistent Claims of Nazi Bases on the Moon and Mars

Vladimir Terziski, President of the American Academy of Dissident Sciences, who has specialized in the study of Nazi rocketry, maintains that the Third Reich landed on the Moon as early as 1942, "utilizing their larger exoatmospheric rocket saucers of the Miethe and Schriever type."

Terziski supports the oft-stated supposition that in the early 1940s, the Nazi scientists were either contacted by an alien culture who presented them with advanced technology or that they reverse engineered a space craft from a crashed UFO. He further claims that as soon as the first German landing party touched down on the Moon, they began digging and tunneling under the surface. By 1944, the Nazis had their first Moon Base.

Another startling revelation from Terziski's research asserts that shortly before World War II ended in 1945, a volunteer suicide crew of German and Japanese blasted off for Mars. Although their saucer-shaped spacecraft crashed on the red planet in January 1946, their advanced life support systems kept them alive until they had constructed a base on Mars.

The Mystery of *Alternative 3*

Such accounts as those above remind one of the controversial *Alternative 3* which was telecast as an alleged documentary on British television in 1977. The script by David Ambrose and Christopher Miles declared that the superpower governments had devised a plan to preserve a tiny nucleus of human survivors. In order to implement its success, many people of high intelligence and expertise in science and technology were being kidnapped and taken to secret bases on the Moon where they served as literal slaves.

According to the supposed documentary, it had been determined by the superpowers that Earth would soon be unable to support life. Our climate's recent strange behavior was only a preview of the tremendous cataclysms to come. The superpowers have been working secretly together in space for decades, and their accomplishments in achieving bases and in conquering the far reaches of planetary travel have advanced far beyond that which has been officially released to the public. Ultrasecret joint U.S. and Russian conferences are held each month in a submarine beneath the Arctic ice cap.

Government agencies around the globe have been kidnapping ordinary people for common labor and turning them into mindless automatons by advanced brainwashing methods. The few reports of NASA astronauts that leaked out concerning strange things sighted on the Moon were suppressed by the secret agencies of the superpowers in order to keep the masses ignorant of the overall sinister plan.

Although the British television program and the later book version of the script by Leslie Watkins, published in 1978, were both decried as science fiction with absolutely no basis in fact, the research of many investigators has produced similarly frightening accusations. Not only are secret agencies of the superpowers portrayed as working together on an overall clandestine master plan, but these same superpowers are accused of having made a deal with intelligences from outer space that has little regard for the average citizen of Earth.

Witnesses who claim top-level security clearances describe the utilization of abandoned U.S. military bases as "interdimensional tunnels," enabling aliens to enter Earth's atmosphere with greater ease. Unspeakable types of experiments with abducted men and women were allegedly conducted. Some witnesses claim that large numbers of street kids and runaways have been used in certain experiments in teleportation of the physical body to established Moon bases.

Mitchell Calls Talk of Moon or Mars Structures Bonkers

On October 11, 1998, the *London Sunday Times* reported astronaut Edgar Mitchell's disclaimers about "little green men" on the Moon. As one of the featured speakers at the UFO Experience Conference in Connecticut, Dr. Mitchell, the sixth man to walk on the lunar surface, doubted alien Moon bases. He did state, however, that he was about 90% certain that among the thousands of UFO reports filed since the late 1940s, a good many remain unexplained. He went on to theorize that "this suggests that there are humanoids manning craft which have characteristics not in the arsenal of any nation on Earth that we know of. That is very alarming."

Dr. Mitchell admitted that until very recently he had been very cautious about making such statements or even about attending UFO conferences. "But now I believe there is sufficient circumstantial evidence to warrant a scientific understanding in this area," he commented. Mitchell's research, which included conversations with people who worked in intelligence agencies and military groups, proves that the U.S. government has been covering up the truth about UFOs for over 50 years. He added:

> The notion that there are structures on Mars or the Moon is bonkers. I can certainly attest to the latter. I've been there [in 1971]. We saw no structures at the landing site and none was reflected in my helmet, as has been alleged.

While we very much admire Dr. Ed Mitchell and like him personally, we must respectfully remind him that he and his fellow astronauts have not actually explored a very large section of the lunar surface. Much of the Moon has not felt the few fateful steps of humankind made by our NASA landing parties.

Is Our Moon an Alien UFO Base?

It was Carl Sagan who conjectured that if extraterrestrial beings had come to observe Earth, they would quite likely establish bases on the Moon and would most logically place their main installations on the "dark side" to keep them safe from probing earthly eyes. If there are alien bases on the Moon, they have probably been there for thousands, if not millions, of years.

The crater Aristarchus is the single brightest spot on the Moon; and at least ever since Galileo began gazing at the area with his telescope in 1610, a wide variety of flares and lights have been reported issuing from that area. Plato, the darkest spot on the Moon, has also been a popular area for changing light patterns to appear. Strange geometrical formations, including luminous triangles and grids of lights have consistently manifested in Plato.

Lights that blink as if sending signals constitute a common lunar phenomenon. The astronomer Webb observed a series of flashing dots and dashes, suggestive of Morse code, on July 4, 1832. On October 20, 1824, European telescopes detected intermittent flashes throughout the night from a dark region near Aristarchus.

In 1873, after conducting an exhaustive study of the blinking lights on the Moon, the Royal Society of Britain issued the candid verdict that the "coded" lunar flashes were "intelligent attempts by an unknown race on the Moon to signal Earth." Those learned men may well have been on to something.

A peculiar facet of the blinking lights is that most of them occur in the northern hemisphere of the Moon. This suggests to some UFO researchers that the extraterrestrial engineers have for some reason found that area to be more suited to expansion.

Strange Objects Sighted Moving Away from the Moon

On September 7, 1820, during a lunar eclipse with the Moon's reflected surface toned down, French astronomers reported strange objects moving in straight lines, separated by uniform distances, moving away from the surface with military precision.

A similar procession of mysterious objects was seen again on August 7, 1869, during a solar eclipse with the Sun's masking glare removed.

In 1874, a Czechoslovakian astronomer claimed that he had seen a dazzling white object traverse the disc of the Moon, then leave the surface and travel out into space.

In 1912, the English astronomer Harris reported that he had seen an "immensely black object about 250 miles long and 150 miles wide" on the Moon. Speculating further, he said that he might have sighted the shadow thrown by something colossal in size moving above the Moon.

In that same year, during a lunar eclipse, both French and British astronomers stated that they had witnessed something like a "superb rocket" shoot away from the surface of the Moon.

Alien Architects or Nature's Jumbled Rocks?

We can only wonder if the boldest—and more imaginative—astronomers have not theorized about the true character of what appear to be works of architecture, rather than rocks randomly jumbled by Nature. Among the hundreds of symmetrical forms there appear to be many that resemble pyramids, cathedrals, great bridges or canals.

Certainly there do exist very strange lunar-formation riddles. For example, where in 1922, did the three mounds in the crater Archimedes suddenly come from? If they are of volcanic origin, as some astronomers state, dismissing the mystery, why was there no red glow or any other signs of violent upheaval in the crater to foreshadow an eruption?

Lunar Bridge

In 1953, while amateur astronomer John J. O'Neill was studying the eastern edge of the Mare Crisium—where, in the previous century, more than 2,000 mysterious lights had been reported—he sighted what appeared to be a large artificial bridge approximately twelve miles long and 500 feet high. At certain angles, sunlight could be seen streaming under the object, clearly demonstrating that it was an arc spanning an area, rather than something lying flat on the lunar surface.

While skeptical professional astronomers could see the so-called bridge, they dismissed it as some sort of natural lunar oddity. They could not explain, however, why that same spot on the Moon had never before exhibited such an arc. And supporting evidence demonstrated that the bridge had not been there five weeks before O'Neill's discovery.

Then two famous English astronomers—Dr. H.P. Wilkins and Patrick Moore—went on a public television program to agree with the amateur astronomer that the bridge most certainly appeared to be artificial. A few months later, Dr. Wilkins himself discovered that near the mysterious lunar bridge was a canyon with perfectly vertical sides and a flat floor, very much like a roadway chiseled out of solid rock and giving the appearance of being connected at one end to the arc itself. "That they should exist side-by-side," Dr. Wilkins said by way of marvelous understatement, "is astonishing."

Lunar Antennae

On November 22, 1966, several of NASA's Surveyor photographs showed a startling series of seven black "spires" that rose up to 70 feet from the Moon's surface and cast clear shadows of what appeared to be machined cones or pyramids.   Scientists examining the photos were so taken aback that one of them blurted out his private thoughts to the ears of the media: "They look like a series of antennas."   Another, following the spontaneous lead of his colleague, added: "They have a deliberate spacing that suggests some sort of planned system."

Very quickly after the inadvertent statements reached the press, the official pronouncement declared the "antennas" to be jagged rocks leaning at such an angle as to produce spire-like shadows.

And so it has been with the Orbiter and Surveyor photographs ever since—millions of photographs that have captured strange geometric shapes that appear to be square, triangular, and even circular in a planned and artificial design.   Can they truly be called random works of Nature?   Or has an unidentified Someone been watching us from our Moon since even before we as a species managed to stand upright?

"Our Home Is Upsilon Bootis"

John A. Keel, a writer who specializes in the unusual, has observed that radio signals of undetermined origin have been flooding Earth's atmosphere since 1899. While scientists and astronomers have now argued for 100 years about the meaning and purpose of these signals, dozens of carefully worded and very explicit messages from some undetermined source have been received all over the planet.

"These messages have been deemed too 'far out' to be accepted by either the scientific Establishment or the press, for they are allegedly from some alien group in outer space," Keel said.

In the 1970s, astronomer Duncan Lunan created a bit of a stir when he announced that he had deciphered a message sent to Earth from another solar system, and he even presented his findings to the prestigious British Interplanetary Society.

Lunan claimed that the message was coming from an unmanned probe robot satellite that had been placed in orbit around our Moon between 13,000 and 15,000 years ago. His research indicated that the device had been transmitting the following message intermittently since the 1920s:

> Start here. Our home is Upsilon Bootis, which is a double star. We live on the sixth planet of seven, counting outward from our sun, which is the larger of the two. Our sixth planet has one moon. Our fourth planet has three. Our first and third planets each have one. Our probe is in the position of Arcturus, known in our maps.

Lunan stated that the computers on the robot probe transmit the message whenever they are triggered by radio waves sent from Earth at an undetermined frequency.

Members of the British Interplanetary Society pointed out that Upsilon Bootis is about 103 million light years from Earth, but the "robot probe" referred to in the message was only about 170,000 miles from our planet, near the Moon, and probably had been set in place about 11,000 BCE. They acknowledged what is commonly known: that radio echoes have been received since the 1920s, but generally ignored because they did not originate on Earth.

Professor Ronald N. Bracewell, one of the leading radio astronomers in the United States, expressed reservations about Lunan's interpretation of the signals, but would not discount them altogether. Indeed, Bracewell had advanced a similar theory to explain radio echoes noted in 1927, 1928, and 1934.

The Monolith on the Moon Scenario

Those readers who are familiar with the motion picture that Stanley Kubrick fashioned from Arthur C. Clarke's *2001: A Space Odyssey*, will certainly recall how the man-apes are intellectually probed and programmed by the aliens' dark, slab-like monolith. Thousands of years later, astronaut pioneers who have established a base on the Moon unearth a still-transmitting monolith. Once the artifact has been uncovered, it begins screaming a signal toward Jupiter that the men-apes of Earth have grown intellectually from leaping from rock to rock to traveling from world to world. Clarke's and Kubrick's 2001 was fiction, but...

On February 14, 1973, the Russian Lunokhod 2 Moon rocket probed an unusual slab of smooth rock that had been blasted into view by a large meteor about a mile from the Taurus Mountains. The meter-long plate, which resembles a modern house panel, proved to be a strong monolith. It has a smooth, seemingly impenetrable surface, while meteorites have pock-marked the giant stones lying nearby.

This monolith may be but the first of several anomalies to be uncovered on the Moon. On the other hand, have we an instance in which science fiction has echoed a future reality? Did Lunokhod 2 discover a clue to other than human intelligence in our universe? And did a signal blast out to another world that our species has begun to approach technological adulthood?

As interesting as that discovery on the Moon may be in its scenario of life reflecting art, it is far more likely that such a signal screamed forth to some other world long before we reached our orbiting satellite. As we examine the ever-amassing evidence, Someone has been watching us for hundreds of thousands of years on an up close and personal basis.

NINE

CROP CIRCLES: COSMIC CLUES FROM THE "OTHER"

Even today, as our advanced civilization careens toward the 21st century, mysterious crop circles continue to be formed and sighted all around the world. Witness this small sampling from the summer of 1998:

- On June 8, a strange kind of circle that could not have been formed by a car or any agricultural machinery was found beside an olive grove on Hvar Otok, a large island just off the coast of Croatia.

- July 22 dawned with a formation consisting of a circle, rings, and pathways measuring 102 feet in diameter, in a wheat field near Providence, Utah.

- In August, crop circle fever broke out in the United Kingdom, appearing in the cornfields of Wiltshire and Hampshire. In a wheat field near Lockeridge in Wiltshire, a complex design of interlocking circles several hundred feet across drew appreciative crowds to inspect the handiwork of unknown artisans.

• Researchers in Germany reported 22 crop circle formations by August.

• On September 14, a counterclockwise circle measuring 11 feet in diameter was found in a wheat field on the outskirts of Wapello, Saskatchewan. A week later, according to Paul Anderson of Circles Phenomenon Research (Canada), a counterclockwise circle measuring 24 feet in diameter was discovered in a wheat field near Spy Hill.

It's Not as Simple as Using a Weed Whacker in a Field

Strange circles or manifestations of unusual geometric designs have been discovered in cereal crops around the world, even in the rice paddies of Japan. The designs are often hundreds of feet in diameter and length and may cover many acres. In nearly all cases, investigators have determined that the crops were biochemically or bio-physically altered.

No one knows how these circles appear as they usually form overnight and are not cut. It is not as simple as some guy going into a field with a weed whacker. While there have been hoaxes, these pranksters have been unable to create crop circles with the same precision and undisturbed nature as those circles thought to be of alien origin.

Why would super-intelligent beings create such objects as crop circles on an increasing basis since 1980? Perhaps there is a strong case that something non-human perpetrates these circles. But whether it proves that these aliens are physical or spiritual is not clear. It is also unclear as to whether they are spiritual with the ability to manifest things in physical form.

Four Theories of Crop Circle Formations

Regardless of a general dismissal of the crop circle phenomenon by conventional scientists who remain skeptical because human beings could be perpetrating hoaxes, it would appear that we do have a genuine mystery in the formation of many of these incredible designs that suddenly appear in fields around the world.

Thus far, the four principal theories regarding the origins of crop circles are the following:

1. Extraterrestrial entities providing clues to their identity and intentions toward Earthlings.

2. Natural phenomena, ranging from insects to lightning, from plasma vortices [a kind of ball lightning] to electromagnetic anomalies.

3. Hoaxsters armed with a length of string and a plank.

4. An ancient non-human intelligence indigenous to earth that is utilizing archetypal designs in order to warn contemporary humankind to be more responsible and more respectful to the planet.

The Sinister Force that Stalked Warminster

The fields of Wiltshire have been prominent in the annals of crop circle research since early in 1966 when journalist Arthur Shuttlewood reported discovering a number of circles 30 feet in diameter that had flattened grass and reeds in a peculiar clockwise fashion. "Saucer nests," as they were called in those days were hardly uncommon. Reports of circular patterns pressed into fields, forest clearings, and marshy areas flooded UFO investigators' offices from Canada to Australia, from the United Kingdom across the United States.

But many long-time researchers remember Shuttlewood tracking what seemed at the time to be a much greater mystery in the nearby market town of Warminster. Beginning on Christmas Day, 1964, residents had reported a strange, paralyzing force that stalked their village.

People told of strange whining and crackling sounds, sinister and menacing vibrations in the air above them. Automobiles stopped abruptly. Men and women walking on the streets reported being relentlessly pressed to the ground by an invisible force.

Representative of such disagreeable encounters would be that of Eric Payne, a young man walking home near the marshland after a date with his girlfriend:

> I heard a loud buzzing. It was not from telegraph wires. It was overhead so quickly that it took me by surprise. As it hovered over me, it sent shivers up my spine. Imagine a giant tin can, filled with huge nuts and bolts, being whirled and rattled above your head. That's how it struck me.

Then something struck me in reality! I felt a series of sharp, stinging blows on my head and
cheeks. A wind tore at my hair and hurt my
eyes. It was so fierce, my head and shoulders
were pressed down, hard. I tried to fight off the
invisible attacker. For some time I staggered
about in the road, then managed to sink to my
knees on a grass verge at the roadside.

Along with such frightening accounts came reports of
brightly glowing objects hovering in the night sky. The
UPI carried the story of a truck driver who sighted
something "of substance" that directed a blinding light
at him while he drove along Westbury Road in Warminster.

It was overhead and shaped like a ball. It was
dancing about. There was a shaft of light like
you would get from a searchlight's beam. It
shook me up all right.

In addition to signs of "saucer nests" and crop circles, the mysterious force in Warminster was also credited with such phenomena as manifesting the sudden
appearance of a spring-fed pool in someone's backyard
to a thistle that grew to the height of twelve feet.

Were the troubled residents of Warminster, often
hailed as England's most haunted village, beset by extraterrestrials, electromagnetic or microwave energy
gone awry, spirits from the beyond, or fairy folk playing
some rather cruel pranks? And whichever force or
phantom was responsible, is it the same one that keeps
on making crop circles?

A Non-Human Intelligence at Work

While English researcher Lucy Pringle believes that many crop circle formations are due to natural causes, such as the discharge of some electromagnetic energy, she also noted that a particular design formed around April 21, 1998 appeared very close to the prehistoric mound of Silbury Hill. She likened the double ringed circle with 33 scroll-like bands between the rings, to a Beltane wheel, an ancient symbol used at Celtic fire festivals on May Day.

A case can be made for the argument that a non-human intelligence is perpetrating these mysterious manifestations, and a very familiar non-human intelligence has played a very significant role in the myths and legends of every known planetary culture for centuries.

The phenomenon of the crop circle is hardly new. Oldtime residents of England speak of the "corn fairies" that made such designs in the fields at the turn of the century. But the manifestation of the crop circle is far older than a mere hundred years or so, for the Germans, the Irish, the Scots, the English, the Scandinavians, and the French have no end of accounts of the discovery of fairy circles dating back to ancient times. We also find variants of these tales in the Slavic countries, in Wales, and in Japan and China.

Native Americans divided their supernatural visitors and companions into two categories: the glowing lights and flying baskets in the sky signaled the arrival of the Star People; and those quick moving little folk who inhabited field and forest were the "vanishing people." And the Native Americans frequently found medicine circles pressed into the grass just as their European counterparts across the ocean found circles that the dancing elves had tromped into the meadows during nocturnal revels.

Cottingly, the Roswell of 1917

Over 80 years ago, two British schoolgirls, Elsie Wright and Frances Griffiths, returned from an outing in the countryside near Cottingly, West Yorkshire. Blithely declaring that they had managed to capture fairies on film, they set in motion a controversy that has never ceased to provoke heated emotions. Sir A. Conan Doyle, the creator of Sherlock Holmes, came to the defense of the girls, for he was convinced that fairies were constructed of energy which emitted vibrations either shorter or longer than the normal spectrum visible to the human eye. People gifted with clairvoyance, such as Elsie Wright and Frances Griffiths, were better able to perceive these vibrations.

In 1998, two feature films based on the Cottingly fairies incident were released for international distribution. *Photographing Fairies* stars Academy Award winner Ben Kingsley and *Fairy Tale: A True Story* casts Peter O'Toole as Sir Arthur Conan Doyle and Harvey Keitel as Harry Houdini. Cottingly was the Roswell of its day, and as producer Michele Camarda (*Photographing Fairies*) said, "We are tapping into the millennium fever, where people are seeking something they cannot find in contemporary religion."

A Strange, Nocturnal Window Peeper

When Brad was a child not quite five years old, he lay on his bed one night and watched out of the window in fascination. His stare was focused on a smallish being that stood on its tip-toes to another window to watch his parents as they moved about the kitchen of their Iowa farm home.

After several moments of enthralled observation on both of their parts, the little being must have felt an uncomfortable sensation of someone watching him:

> He turned to look at me over his shoulder and I got a good look at his tiny, pinched features in the light from the kitchen window. It seemed as if he gave me a conspiratorial smile, as if we were sharing a secret that was at once both profound and simple. I am not certain exactly what happened next, but it seemed that his face came nearer and nearer to my own—and then he vanished.
>
> I am able to discuss this experience quite intellectually and "explain" it in approved psychological terms. I am prepared to regard the episode as the single most vivid dream of my childhood. At the time, though, I was convinced that I had seen a fairy, a brownie, an elf. And I must confess, regardless of my ready facade of sophistication toward the matter, I still believe that on that October night 57 years ago I was given my own personal evidence of the Other—a non-human intelligence that may have been terrestrial, extraterrestrial, or multidimensional in origin. And it was that sighting, along with a near-death-experience when I was eleven, that set me on my quest of exploring the unexplained.

Perhaps what such seemingly disparate phenomena as the UFO, the appearance of fairies, the visitations of angels, and the manifestation of strange crop circles throughout the world really mean is that we are part of a large community of intelligences. Perhaps we exist as part of a complex hierarchy of powers and principalities, a universe of interrelated species—both physical and nonphysical.

Since his childhood experience with the Other, Brad's work as an author of the paranormal has brought him into contact with many adult men and women who have privately admitted that they have seen fairies, UFO beings, Devas, and nature spirits. Somewhere along the path of his research, Brad came across this interesting quote from Herman Hesse in his *Autobiographical Writings* that led him to ponder if there were not thousands, possibly millions, of people who were aware of their non-human companions:

> ...I do not know when I saw him for the first time: I think he was always there, that he came into the world with me. The little man was a tiny, gray, shadowy being, a spirit or goblin, angel or demon, who at times walked in front of me in my dreams as well as during my waking hours, and whom I had to obey, more than my father, more than my mother, more than reason, yes, often more than fear.

An Ancient Race of Beings, Neither Divine nor Human

The noted medium Eileen J. Garrett, in her book *Many Voices*, remarks that she tended toward a belief in fairies and speaks of the older country people who claimed to have seen them. In her opinion, "this ancient belief in a race of beings neither divine or human, existing apart on a "plane" different from humans but occupying the same space, tended to give one a perpetual sense of never being alone."

Traditionally, fairies are an ancient race of beings, the counterparts of humankind in person, but at the same time, nonphysical or multidimensional. They are mortal in existence, but lead longer lives than their human cousins.

In *all* traditions, from England to Scandinavia and throughout the globe, the fairy folk are depicted as strongly dependent on human beings, and from time to time they seek to reinforce their own kind by kidnapping humans. Although they are of a nature between spirits and humans, they can intermarry and bear children.

Since the beginning of time, the human race and the ultra-dimensional race of fairies have shared this planet, experiencing a strange, symbiotic relationship.

One of those remarkable cross-cultural references is *Puckwudjini,* an Algonquin word, commonly used among many Native American tribes, which signifies "little vanishing people." Perhaps this is also Shakespeare's "sweet Puck" who chuckles about how foolish we mortals be.

From Puck in England we cross the waters to find *Puke,* a generic name for minor spirits in all the Teutonic and Scandivanian dialects. Puke is cognate with · the German *spuk,* a goblin; and the Dutch, spook, a frightening ghost. There is also, of course, the Irish *pooka* and the Cornish *Pixie.*

Separate the suffix of Puckwudjini and we are left with *jini,* the Mid_east's wish-granting inhabitant of magical lamps.

Interestingly, we have the Other revealing itself around the world as Puck—from American Indian tribes to Nordic tribes to African tribes. And universally, we have precisely the same kinds of human and fairy interaction with the same game plays, the same purposes, the same lessons to be learned.

For centuries, an awareness of such entities impressed upon those men and women who lived next to the land that there are "sacred" areas that must not be violated.

It would seem that the ancient non-human intelligence communicates with us essentially through the subconscious mind. That is why experiences with non-human intelligence happen more often, and most effectively, when one is in an altered state of consciousness—and that is why UFO experiences, fairyland adventures, angelic visitations, and so forth, sound so much like dreams. These experiences really occur during a dreamlike state. The conscious mind of the percipient remembers certain highlights of the experience, or interprets the symbols and lessons in a consciously acceptable manner. The actual teaching mechanism and the important information have been indelibly etched upon the subconscious.

When the late psychic-sensitive Olof Jonsson spoke of his childhood "playmates," he may well have been making an astute observation about the deeper levels of interacting with non-human intelligence:

> These beings may have been the same entities that so often represent themselves to small children as fairies and wood sprites.... But somehow, on occasion, I believe that I was able to see them as they really were...It was they who began to tell me wonderful things about the universe and cosmic harmony...I felt that they were friends, that they wanted to teach me and to help me.

...I am still convinced that these beings are friendly and intend to help humankind as much as they can without interfering in our own development and free will.

All of Nature Is Infused with Divine Intelligence

In the summer of 1970, Dorothy Maclean of the Findhorn Trust community in northern Scotland, received the insight that "all of nature was infused with the divine intelligence which was embodied by beings living on higher vibratory dimensions from the physical." These beings were the Deva (in Sanskrit, "shining ones"), elementals or nature spirits, of an order of evolution existing parallel to humanity. They wielded forces that could energize and externalize the processes and forms of nature; and they warned that too many citizens of the Western world had lost their sense of oneness with nature, thereby greatly increasing the danger of destroying the world.

However, the Devas promised, in the new cycle that is dawning, humanity will once again learn to live in harmony with all life forms on the planet. A short time later, the folks at Findhorn became world famous for producing marvelous vegetables and fruits out of formerly barren and infertile soil.

David Spangler, a community director, once said that the nature beings were primarily concerned about the maintenance of harmony and wholeness on Earth. Since humanity as a species is a necessary and vital part of the synergistic state, the health of humanity is of concern, because it reflects the health of the planet.

Understanding the Cosmic Clues

Many people are coming to realize that we have muted our mystical communion with Mother Earth. We have grown apart from our sense of Oneness with the God-Force that pervades all things. Perhaps we are now receiving cosmic clues such as crop circles around us to give us an opportunity to regain symbolically that state of union that we miss so terribly.

It would be foolish to apply primitive modes of action in our contemporary society or to engage in superstitious practices in an attempt to stop the world and establish a separate reality. However, focusing on the clues presented to us in the form of the crop circles may permit us to deal directly with the unconscious and to make firm contact with the archetypal psyche. Many wise spiritual teachers have expressed their opinion that modern humanity desperately needs to apprehend that level of consciousness that understands existence as an organic whole.

To be primitive in our interaction with the external world of consensual reality is, indeed, to live in superstition and confusion. To be primal in our interaction with the inner-world of the psyche is to live in wisdom and in spiritual balance.

TEN

NATIVE AMERICAN BELIEFS:
THE RETURNING POWER

Although many historians and anthropologists believe that the Native American people buried their spirit as well as their hearts at Wounded Knee and that the contest between the whiteman's religion and the redman's medicine was decided along with the issues of territories and treaties, the late 1960s began to witness a dramatic rebirth of the strength and the spirit of tribal belief structures.

For many years the old ways and traditions had been carefully nurtured and quietly cherished, but medicine power would now return in a manner that would reveal our Native American heritage as laded with spiritual insights fraught with special meaning for our new age of ever-rising awareness.

In the 1990s, individual Native American Medicine Priests have been speaking out as never before. Information that previously has been secretly and sacredly passed only from prophet to prophet is now being shared with all who will listen, all who will treat the knowledge with respect, all who will, hopefully act wisely upon it.

A great deal of the long-held secret knowledge of the tribal shamans has to do with information about devastating earthquakes, famine, floods, and other major changes in our physical environment that will "shake us awake." As the shamans all declare, we are living in the most important time in all of history.

The Second Coming of the White Buffalo Woman

Many medicine practitioners believe that an omen of the acceleration of time manifested in the miracle of the white buffalo calf that was born at a farm in Janesville, Wisconsin, in 1994. Floyd Hand, a Sioux medicine priest from Pine Ridge, South Dakota, stated that to the traditions of many Native Americans, "This is like the Second Coming of Christ."

According to ancient tradition, the White Buffalo Woman appeared during a time of great famine. She presented the Lakota with a sacred pipe with which to pray and taught them the value of the buffalo. The late Dallas Chief Eagle translated her words as they have been passed down for many generations:

> I was here before the rains, the snows, and the hail. I was here before the mountains and the winds. I am the spirit of Nature. I am in the light that fills the earth, and in the darkness of night-time. I give color to nature, for I am in nature's

growth and fruits. I am again in nature where
themes of mystic wisdom are found.
I am in your chants and laughters. I am in the
tears that flow from sorrow. I am in the bright
joyous eyes of the children. I am in the substance
that gives unity, completeness, and oneness. I
am in you when you walk the simple path of the
red man.

I am in you when you show love of humankind,
for I also give love to those who are loving. I am
in the response of love among all humans, for
this is a path that will find the blessing and fulfillment of the Great Mystery.

I must leave you now to appear in another age,
but I leave you with the red man's path.

Now such medicine priests as Floyd Hand say that
the spirit of the White Buffalo Woman has returned to
warn us of the disasters to come and to rescue the
world from destruction. Hand said that the White
Buffalo Woman appeared to him in a dream and promised that on the 21st day of the 21st year in the 21st
century we will achieve paradise. But for the next 23
years, we can expect some very difficult times.
Hand was specific about these times:

There will be a new respect for one another and
the Earth and those who continue to destroy the
Earth will soon kill each other off. Many of our
cities will be wiped out by natural disasters and
skyscrapers will be replaced by trees. Our future
will more greatly resemble our past. We may still
have some modern conveniences, but they'll run

on environmentally sound fuels. We will turn to the Sun for our energy, and the Earth will be able to heal.

Thunder Beings Are Truth Beings

Grandmother Twylah of the Seneca is one of the most revered Medicine priests who have shared knowledge and wisdom in this coming time of cleansing and initiation. She foresees dramatic changes that will occur before the end of this century, and she envisions great cosmic beings that are gathering to assist humankind through this terrible time of transition.

"Thunder Beings are truth beings," she said, referring to these powerful entities that offer humans their assistance. "Their teachings are of truth, and they are filled with love. In these final days, it is important to think of unconditional love and not to permit anything to interfere."

Twylah believes that the Thunder Beings are now speaking to everyone, "but only the awakened Thunder People are listening." In order to hear the Thunder Beings, she gave firm advice: "Go within...go within...go within. Go within to your vital core."

Rolling Thunder's Search for the Thunder People

During the last thirty years of his life, the great Shoshone-Cherokee Medicine priest Rolling Thunder sought those balanced men and women who could rightfully bear the mantle of Thunder People. In his opinion, expressed often before his death in the winter of 1997, it will be the Thunder People who will be on a level of awareness high enough to assist others during the coming times of planetary purification and transformation.

Thunder, he explained, in the ancient mythologies of Scandinavia, Greece, and the Native American tribes, means "telling the truth." Rolling Thunder maintained that the true Thunder People could put their minds together as one "to believe in truth, justice, and peace."

The great Medicine priest suffered greatly from pain of the spirit over all the violence that permeates the land and the terrible sins that have been visited upon the Earth Mother. Speaking of the future, he said:

> Thunder People will seek to straighten things out in peaceful ways. If enough people prefer peace, there will be peace. If the next war is allowed to happen, there will be no winners. If one of us suffers, we are all going to suffer.

Ghost Wolf Also Hears the Thunders

Robert Ghost Wolf also hears the "Thunders." He states that the spirits decree that humankind isn't being condemned, but is being given a chance to react to problems in different ways. He does relay warnings of starvation and illness for human beings and bizarre mutations of animals.

While we are definitely heading toward the end times, Ghost Wolf states that the forthcoming difficult conditions do not portend the end of the world. We humans have brought about the hard days to come because of our own errant behavior.

"The earth is a living organism," he said. "She has her own consciousness, her own plans, dreams, future, and needs.   The earth will continue to go on—but whether we choose to go on with it, that's the question."

Discerning Guardian Beings from Destroyers

The late Sun Bear, the powerful Chippewa shaman and founder of the Bear Tribe, acknowledged that while the Medicine priests were the living guardians of the Earth Mother, there existed spirit beings who were the guardians and protectors over them. At the same time, Sun Bear warned, there were also spirits of destruction hovering about all of us:

> These destroyers will soon unleash their entire strength. The only people who retain their balance will be the people who have linked into their minds the things that are really solid and true. These people will survive because they will keep themselves away from the centers of strife and destruction.

Other Worlds Before Ours Have Been Destroyed

All of the Native American tribes repeat legends that tell of their people emerging from the destruction that had been visited upon a former civilization on the North American continent. Further, all of the Medicine priests issue warnings that the present world will be destroyed if humankind cannot achieve a higher level of responsibility toward Mother Earth and all of her life forms.

The Seneca prophets say that the world has undergone the traumatic experiences of birth, death, and rebirth six times before. They predict that all of humanity now stands on the brink of destruction prior to entering the final world in our evolutionary cycle.

The Hopi traditionalists state that we will enter the final world after we have endured a last great war that will have to do with a "spiritual conflict with material matters." After the great struggle has been resolved, spirit beings will remain "to create one world and one nation under one power, that of the Creator Spirit."

In Frank Water's *Book of the Hopi,* we read that the emergence to the future Fifth World has begun:

> It is being made by the humble people of little nations, tribes, and racial minorities...Plant forms from previous worlds are beginning to spring up as seeds...The same kinds of seeds are being planted in the sky as stars. The same kinds of seeds are being planted in our hearts. All these are the same, depending how you look at them. That is what makes the Emergence to the next, Fifth World.

Hopi Elders Speak on National Radio

As evidence of an increased willingness on the part of traditional Medicine priests to share their wisdom with all receptive men and women, two Hopi Elders spoke frankly of the Time of Purification that lies ahead for the planet. [*Coast to Coast,* June 17, 1998] For their own protection, they asked to be identified only as Grandmother and Grandfather. Among their prophecies for the End Times were the following warnings:

- World War III will take place with much world starvation.

- World weather will become increasingly erratic.

- Many Earth changes and catastrophes will occur as they have in centuries past.

- The animals will begin to turn on humans. There will be many animal attacks all across North America and the world.

- Those men and women who have chosen to walk on the dark side and practice evil will be eliminated. Only those who are walking on the path of oneness and have a good heart will be spared in the time of great cleansing that lies ahead.

Ancient Prophecies Warn of the Great Cleansing

Ancient Incan prophecies preserved by the Q'uero shamans of the Peruvian Andes predict the end of time as we now perceive it, but they optimistically foresee a new golden age emerging after dramatic Earth changes. While they envision the general collapse of European culture, they also see the new caretakers of Earth as being symbolically structured with North America providing the body, Europe, the head, and South America, the heart.

Mayan prophecies may have set a date for the cleansing and/or destruction of the present world. According to Adrian Gilbert and Maurice Cotterell in their book, *The Mayan Prophecies*, the Mayan calendar prophesies the end of our own "Age of the Jaguar" and foresees the fifth and final Sun in 2012. We don't have long to wait to judge the accuracy of this ancient prophecy.

The Great Purification Is Necessary for Spiritual Growth

In the various philosophies of the Medicine priests, there is a general agreement that the destruction of the previous worlds has been a necessary aspect of humankind's spiritual evolution and growth.

Sadly, according to the shaman's viewpoint, humans too easily forget the lessons of the Great Mystery and fall away to rely upon their own feeble—and often self-destructive—devices. When such a state of affairs comes to pass, the Great Mystery causes a time of Great Purification, which cleanses the Earth Mother and creates a new and pure environment for a new epoch, a new world.

Sun Bear agreed that it might be a difficult concept for many to comprehend, but he maintained that the changes forthcoming in the Great Purification are necessary:

If the corrections that result from [the Great Purification] aren't made, then those people who don't have a true sense of balance could succeed in destroying the Earth, probably contaminating it beyond any chance of recovery. I see the Earth changes as positive, because they are necessary for the survival of the planet. If humanity is going to survive these changes, we will have to develop a much higher consciousness. Such a change will be very positive and good for all of creation.

We Can Prepare for Coming Earth Changes

The great Medicine priests are all saying that another time of purification and cleansing has rolled around on the great cosmic calendar. We are once again about to enter a time of earthquakes, volcanisms, and dramatic Earth changes. And while these prophets advise us that there is nothing that we can do to prevent the cataclysms before us, we can prepare for them.

Grandmother Twylah has said that the year 1991 was the year of challenge and 1992 was the year of change. Our year of choice was 1993, and 1994 was the year of commitment:

> The year 1995 brought so many changes for so many people that it no longer made any difference how much they knew about what lies ahead. It is now time that people better get on their horses and decide which direction they're going. The important thing will be whether or not they will be able to stand in their truth. Those who stand in their truth will eat whatever Mother Nature provides—and it will be roots, bark, and seeds. Before this decade ends, we will be crawling on our bellies—but we will be surviving.

Twylah warns that the "great fires" have already begun burning:

> The Middle East set the flames going. The planet is warming up; the ice is melting, so much land is going to go under. The Earth Mother is changing her garments. She's going to put on some new stuff. She is going to be dancing around. And

it's about time. She's sick and tired of the way she's been treated.

Twylah repeated the importance of standing in one's truth during the troubled times ahead:

Supposing right at this moment the Earth began to quake and up in the sky world there would be thunder and lightning and so much noise that we couldn't think. The best thing that we could do for our survival would be to stand on our truth. To run in panic never accomplishes anything.

Prophecies Help Us Wake Up

Mary Elizabeth Thunder has said:

Prophecies are given to us as possible outcomes if we don't wake up and participate in the change. Seeds of a new consciousness are raining down on the planet, very much like the time when the human race was formed here on Earth millions of years ago. Now Mother Earth is pregnant again, and she is birthing a New Dimension, so we as a race do not have a great deal of time to raise our consciousness to be in tune with the Oneness of Universal Truth.

Mary is part Cheyenne, part Mohawk, part Irish, and adopted Lakota. In 1981, she suffered a heart attack and underwent an afterlife experience. During her recovery, many highly respected tribal shamans advised her to focus on her work as a teacher.

Recalling Rolling Thunder's observation that the true pollution on Earth comes from the minds of humans, Mary determined that:

> We must make our lives spiritual twenty-four hours a day. We must eat and drink natural foods and liquids. We must give up drugs and other poisons to our systems that only confuse, dull, and degenerate the mind and body.

In Mary Thunder's view, we are at the time of illumination for Planet Earth:

> We have a message of healing from the Sun behind the Sun. It is healing in a balanced way: the male/female, the positive/negative, the Father Sun/Mother Earth. The Native Americans were always the ones with secrets of "grounding" and of balancing opposing forces. We must return to the natural ways. We must sincerely learn that we are a part of All That Is. Mother Earth is within us, and we are within her.

> We can recognize ourselves as vehicles of the Great Mystery, and we can return to the original instructions of spiritual laws for guidance. We can learn to heal with the natural medicines of pure air, clean water, fertility, and solar rays.

Q'uero shamans believe that the doorways between the worlds are opening right now and present literal "holes in time" through which we might enter and more fully explore our human capabilities. It is possible to regain the luminous nature with which humankind was originally blessed.

Honor Nature and the Spiritual Laws of Old

On the summer solstice in 1988, representatives of the Incas, the Aztecs, and many North American tribal priests gathered together to make the announcement of the dawning of a new era. In order to prosper during this time of rebirth, humankind must return to the natural way of living and remember the spiritual laws of old. As Mary Elizabeth Thunder reminds us:

> Native people believe that all children—all of us— come from one father and one mother—Father Sun and Mother Earth—so we are all brothers and sisters. All blood is the same color, the color of living fire. All nations of the world from the beginning have had the same natural flag: the rainbow. The people of the Earth Mother are like a bouquet of flowers—different colors, but all the same, beautiful in a bouquet.
>
> The heart of the Sun is open for all of us to heal ourselves and Mother Earth. The time for choice, for all of us, is right now. Pray for the people so the people might live.

ELEVEN

MILLENNIAL PROPHECY
AND THE COMING EARTH CHANGES

We are basically living on a thin crust atop a mostly molten globe, so is it any wonder that we are so drastically affected by the changes in the Earth—or that we are so concerned with trying to predict what is going to happen to us? With the various cracks and crevices in our globe, we are besieged by cataclysmic volcanic eruptions and violent earthquakes, more now, it seems, than ever before.

What we need to realize is that there are forces around us that we have no way of controlling. We cannot stop the force of a hurricane that destroys a coastal town, we cannot stop a whirling tornado that whips a building from its foundation as if it was made of matchsticks. The solid ground underneath our feet and the sky above our heads have surprises in store for us, in greater quantities now than ever before.

Many seers and researchers attribute the increase in catastrophic quakes and eruptions to the fast approaching days of the Millennium.

Americans Always Fascinated by Apocalypse

Millennial thought dates back to the ancient Persian philosophers; but as a people, Americans seem always to have been fascinated by the horror of a certain strain of apocalyptic thought. The dark fear that the Book of Revelation with its grim visions of plagues and catastrophes would come to pass and that the world as we know it will come to an end—along with a day of awful judgment for our species—has always held us in its grasp.

Indeed, the very discoverer of the New World, Christopher Columbus, was a devout reader of biblical prophecies and believed that the world would come to an end in 1650. He perceived his founding of a new continent to be part of God's divine plan to establish a millennial paradise to house those who survived the final battle between Good and Evil that would take place midway through the 17th century. He believed that God had anointed him to serve as a special messenger of the new heaven and the new earth which were prophesied in the Apocalypse of St. John in the Book of Revelation.

After Columbus himself set a profound example, hundreds of American preachers from Colonial times through the Civil War and up to the present day have occupied themselves with predicting the exact time of Christ's Second Coming. And those earnest followers who have occupied the pews of their churches, as well as a sizable number of those who never set foot in a formal place of worship, have believed that Jesus' return to Earth was imminent.

Even Edgar Allan Poe, who more often occupied himself with dank pits, tell-tale hearts, and foul murders, seemingly overdosed on the Book of Revelation. Poe joined America's obsession with the apocalypse by writing a story entitled, "The Conversation of Eiros and Charmion," that envisions the world ending when a deadly comet approaches Earth.

For a period of about a week, Poe writes, the approach of the comet seemed nothing particularly out of the ordinary, but then a violent light suddenly penetrates all things:

> Let us bow down...before the excessive majesty of the great God! There came... shouting and pervading sound, as if from the mouth of HIM.... The whole incumbent mass of ether in which we existed burst at once into a species of intense flame, for whose surpassing brilliancy and all-fervid heat even the angels in the high Heaven of pure knowledge have no name. Thus ended all.

In November 1997, a *U.S. News* poll indicated that 66% of Americans—including a third of those who profess to be non-churchgoers—believe that Jesus Christ will appear one day in the clouds with a host of angels announcing His Second Coming. Interestingly, that percentage is up five points from a previous poll determining public attitude about the return of Jesus.

Echoes of Our Planet's Future Death?

Harold Bloom, author of *Omens of the Millennium,* suggests our fascination with the millennium may have something to do with "our obsession with individual mortality. It's hard for all of us to understand that we will go and everything will still be here."

Indeed, the apocalyptic messages that have been so very much a part of humankind's history of prophecy may be the result of the echo of the inevitable death of our planet, which, for us, lies somewhere in the undetermined future. During altered states of consciousness, a prophet may rise to the consciousness of the Eternal Now where he can see all of history as a whole. His heightened perspective may enable him to see the demise of our planet as an event that affects everyone who has ever lived on Earth.

All of humankind will share in the loss of Earth's art, music, literature, sculpture, architecture, science, and philosophy. These human-stamped tangible and intangible artifacts comprise the legacy left to the children of the first parents as well as to the unborn on that unnamed day when the Sun dies. If history is truly cyclical, as we suspect it is, then the end will never be far from the beginning, regardless of the centuries of linear time in between.

What Awaits Us in the Next Millennium?

What can we expect to happen to our nation, our world, our universe as we move inexorably toward the next millennium?

Many scholars and researchers have attempted to correlate the messages from the Bible with the end of the Piscean Age and the advent of the Age of Aquarius.

At the same time, millions of desperately worried men and women care little about the philosophy or the divergent theologies of the Millennium. They are concerned only whether the vast geographical, climatic, and societal changes predicted for the planet in the next few years will actually come to pass.

Can we expect the chaos and destruction predicted by so many seers over the ages to bring about the end of the world as we know it? Will mountain ranges and coastlines rise and fall along with governments and political structures? Will those who survive a terrible time of cleansing be blessed with enlightenment and ascension to a higher plane of existence?

Tracing the Origin of Millennial Thought

While the Second Coming of Jesus Christ is referred to over 300 times in the New Testament, the Millennium is mentioned only five times—and all in sequential verses in Revelation 20:2-7:

And he [Christ] seized the dragon...which is the Tempter and Satan...and bound him a thousand years, and cast him into the bottomless pit and shut him up...that he should no more deceive the nations until the thousand years be past...And I saw thrones and those who sat upon them, and judgment was given to them.... And I saw the souls of them who had not worshipped the beast...nor had received his mark upon their foreheads or their hand; and lived and reigned with Christ a thousand years...Blessed and holy is he who has part in the first resurrection; over such the second death has no power, but they

will be the priests of God and of Christ, and they
shall reign with him a thousand years. And
when the thousand years come to an end, Satan
shall be loosed out of his prison.

Thus we have the most enigmatic Book in the Bible
providing scant scriptural references to the most mysterious and momentous event ever prophesied. And because so much of the Millennium mystery remains
open to speculation, it should come as no surprise that
the number of prophecies about what many consider to
be the climatic event in human history are both plen-
tiful and dramatic.

The Climatic Struggle Between Good and Evil

For many people worldwide, the predictions in the
Book of Revelation foresee the End Times of Planet
Earth. These times shall culminate in Armageddon, the
last great battle between the Forces of Light and the
Forces of Darkness, and terminate with Christ's victory
over Satan and the subsequent Day of Judgment.

Certain Christian fundamentalists believe in that last
great battle so fervently that Jerusalem police reported
in October 1998, that they were already having difficulty with American religious zealots who are coming to
the Holy Land to witness and welcome the arrival of
Armageddon. Many born-again Christians have already
moved into homes and hotel rooms near the Mount of
Olives. Israeli officials stated that they know of three
groups of fundamentalist Christians who are in the
process of selling all their belongings so that they may
be in Jerusalem when Jesus returns.

Rather than a climatic battle between the forces of good and evil, the Native American prophets say that what we are really predicting is a fast-approaching Time of Great Cleansing that is about to purify and to reconsecrate the Earth Mother.

Such a cleansing may occur horribly through the purgation of nuclear fire. Vast numbers of the human population may be eliminated through a terrible disease, and the entire face of Mother Earth will be altered through earthquakes, volcanoes, and massive internal upheavals.

Hopi Ancient Prophecies Are Right on Schedule

White Bear of the Hopi once echoed the words of Jesus when he stated that those who are humble would inherit the Earth. "There are two forces in this Universe," he said. "Those who destroy, and those whose spiritual power is trying to reach humankind."

White Bear declared that the ancient people of the Hopi are the people of non-aggression who have never declared war on anybody. For centuries they have been blessed with a tablet that tells the story of what is going to take place in the universe:

> The ancient prophecies are right on schedule. If the Great Plan says that there will be a catastrophe tomorrow, there is nothing that we can do to postpone this to another day. It is time now that all those people who have awareness, the true light, must see the truth and be aggrieved.

White Bear went on to say that the Hopis had knowledge of the destruction of the first, second, third, and fourth worlds, centuries and centuries ago:

> In my tribe, our people have a two horn society, the custodians of the history of our knowledge. The horn on the right sees all knowledge that lies ahead. The horn on the left sees all knowledge that has passed. We know where we came from and we know where we are going. We know how the world was formed and that it will be destroyed by fire again. That is why we live in old Oraibi, Arizona, a place where atomic radiation has never fallen.

An Opportunity to Transcend Our Humanness

There are those mystics who foresee dramatic Earth changes as a violent period of planetary cleansing that will herald a time of transition for the entire human species, a quantum leap forward in humankind's evolution. Those who endure will have the opportunity to undergo the metamorphosis from *Homo sapiens* to *Homo spiritus*. And for many of these visionaries, the Millennium will usher in an additional opportunity to rise to higher awareness in fellowship with entities from other worlds or other universes.

ETs Say Earth Must Undergo a Cleansing

An extraterrestrial entity calling itself OX-HO told the Light Affiliates of British Columbia that the great Earth changes were inevitable: "Your world is contaminated to the very core. Earth must be cleansed."

Once the cleansing has occurred, OX-HO promised, humans would be eligible to make a transition into a whole new dimension of being:

There is a whole new world waiting for you people of Earth...one of subtleties, of lighter shades of beauty. With your increased vibrations, you will be able to see these subtleties more intensely than you have imagined. As we said, your Earth will be stepped up in frequency and vibration to the next level. Be one with this vibration, you will become a different person from the old you.

Aleuti Francesca, a mystic and channeler of Space Brothers, states that we must recognize that our true "home" is that of the inner world where we may achieve greater attunement with the god-self.

Although the cycle of Earth time may be growing shorter with accompanying dramatic Earth changes, her extraterrestrial contacts informed Ms. Francesca that we should accept this time as an opportunity for a reassessment of our values:

Earthman must meet himself face to face. A time is coming for the ending of a cycle and the beginning of a new; and at this time, Earthman meets Spaceman in the one light and under the one Sun of this universe.

Whitley Strieber received a visitation from an entity in Toronto in June 1998. Identifying himself as a messenger from a "higher world," the being informed Strieber that our world was "irretrievably lost." When Strieber asked if the "Visitors" might not intervene, the entity said that they would not. Earth was destined to undergo a time of great agony, but those humans "on the path" would find their way through the maelstrom.

Millennium Prophecies from Many Sources

John Harper writes: "In the best prophecies 60% is man, 40% is God. In the usual prophecies 90% is man, 10% is God."

Ancient prophecies, as well as contemporary seership, provide us with some very frightening scenarios of what may lie ahead for us during the Time of Cleansing.

On one thing all prophets seem to agree: We are in for some very difficult years ahead. The final years of this century and the next decade will, indeed, be the "best of times and the worst of times."

The great prophet Nostradamus said that an angel divinely inspired his prophecies. Authorities on the 16th century seer appear to agree that only one of the prophetic quatrains still to be realized contains a date, "the year 1999, the seventh month." At that time, with Saturn providing the signal, there will be famine, cataclysms, plague, economic turmoil, and warfare.

Predictions from Edgar Cayce, "Sleeping Prophet"

Edgar Cayce, the famous "sleeping prophet" of Virginia Beach, made many of his predictions of the coming millennium in the 1930s. He foresaw events that would begin in the late 1950s, reach a kind of climax in the late 1990s, then continue through the year 2000 and beyond. Among those glimpses of the future are such dire predictions as the following:

- Earth will be broken up in the western portion of America.

- The greater portion of Japan will go into the sea.

- Land will appear off the East Coast of America.

- There will be upheavals in the Arctic and in the Antarctic that will set off the eruption of volcanoes in the Torrid Zone. Such action may even cause the shifting of the poles so that formerly frigid or semitropical regions will become warmer and more tropical in nature.

- There will be new lands seen off the Caribbean Sea.

- South America will be shaken from the uppermost portion to the southernmost tip.

- Large portions of Los Angeles and San Francisco will be destroyed.

- Due to the reactivation of the volcanoes Vesuvius and Pelee, the southern coast of California and the areas between Salt Lake City and the southern portion of Nebraska may expect an inundation within three months.

When Cayce was asked while in a trance what humankind might do to prepare for such dramatic Earth changes, he replied:

Do thy duty today. Tomorrow will take care of itself. These changes in the Earth will come to pass, for the time and the times and half times are at an end [see the Book of Revelation 12:14; Daniel 7:25, 12:7], and there begin these periods for the readjustments. For how hath He given? "The righteous shall inherit the Earth."

The New Jerusalem Awaits Those Who Survive

You can perceive the end result of the global cleansing process as an opportunity for the transcendental transformation of our species or as the Second Coming of Christ and his victory over Satan. Overall, the trick is somehow to survive antichrists, earthquakes, famine, pestilence, wars, erupting volcanoes, crashing mountains, and vanishing coastal shorelines.

The vast majority of millennial prophecies agree that for those who do manage to survive Armageddon, the final reward justifies whatever struggles must be endured. The attainment of the New Jerusalem is the fulfillment of God's ancient covenant with humankind.

No more dissension will exist among Earth's inhabitants, no more negativity and no more attacks from the Powers of Darkness. Humans will no longer experience physical death or pain as the curse of the human condition is lifted. Overall, there will be no more interference from satanic energies in our species evolution. The Tree of Life will reappear and—the ultimate promise—God's true presence will be revealed.

Truly, humankind's sojourn on Earth appears to be a great odyssey, as once again all people shall emerge in new, glorified bodies, free to roam the limitless spheres of space, at one with God and the Universe.

A Potpourri of Millennium Prophecies

Before we attain that promised New Jerusalem, it appears that we cannot avoid some very difficult times. Here is a brief sampler of the kind of predictions that are being made today by various seers, prophets, channelers, and UFO contactees:

- Israel is being lured into a false peace by those who seek to compromise its security. There will be a great power struggle centered in the Holy Land. Millions of people will die in the most devastating war of all history.

- Colossal tidal waves will hit California and other countries by the second quarter of the year 2000.

- Atlantis will rise from the Atlantic near Bimini Island in the Bahamas.

- There will be a series of drastic U.S. dollar devaluations beginning from the year 1998 to 2000 and beyond.

- A major blackout will affect the entire world during Christmas 1999. Although scientists will attempt to come up with an explanation, it will have been caused by angelic forces.

- Hurricanes, floods, and other natural catastrophes will continue to get worse. Winters will get dramatically colder, causing unprecedented damage throughout the world.

- International terrorism will shatter the United States in 1999 with a rash of bombings and violence in our cities.

- The world as we know it will end on August 13, 2000, but it will continue in some other form.

- Two Suns shall appear in our solar system.

- Another U.S. President will be assassinated.

- The Antichrist will come from Mesopotamia [Iraq]. Blood will paint the swords of the good and the evil. Fire will engulf the masses as smoke rises to the heavens. Christ's soldiers mount a defense against the blades of Satan's warriors. For the faithful, the price will be high, but persistence and patience will bring rewards of rejoicing and everlasting peace with the Lord as He promised.

- In 2077, hundreds of thousands of the inhabitants of Earth will leave the planet and migrate to another.

THE COMING EARTH CHANGES

We shall now focus our examination on the prophecies concerning imminent Earth changes. While there will, of course, be those who lament the passing of the old world, many others will rejoice that a new world is being born.

The Visions of Gordon-Michael Scallion

Gordon-Michael Scallion began receiving visions of future Earth changes while he was recovering from a health crisis in 1979. When a rising percentage of the predictions began to be realized, Scallion knew that he must heed the voice that had charged him to "warn the people." Scallion publishes a monthly newsletter, *The Earth Changes Report*, in which he endeavors to keep people informed concerning his glimpses of the future.

Scallion has received a great deal of attention for the large colored map of the United States that he released in 1993. The map depicts the U.S. as he visualizes it in the years 1998-2001 after massive earthquakes change the world.

In his visions, Scallion has foreseen a mega earthquake in California that will register 10 points or higher on the Richter Scale. This super-quake will fracture a line from Eureka down to Baja. Huge gaps and fissures will run the length of the San Joaquin and Sacramento valleys, creating floods that will inundate much of the central portion of the state.

By 1999, as the North American plate heaves violently upward, a second fracture will cause most of the state of California to sink under the sea. Higher points of elevation throughout the state will remain as islands.

Sometime just before 1999, Scallion envisions the plates shifting to cause a large landmass to break away west of a line running from Newport, Oregon to Tucson, Arizona. The city of Phoenix will become a major seaport on this newly created western coastline.

Between 1998 and 2001, the final major shift will occur, and the greater portion of the land mass west of a line from southwest Nebraska to northeast Arizona will be submerged. The formerly inland states of Nebraska, Wyoming, and Colorado will now become coastal areas.

The Eastern seaboard will not escape earthquake activity during this period. Scallion foresees much of the East Coast, from New York to Florida, inundated and reduced in elevation. At least 50% of the present shoreline will be reduced, and people will begin to move inland in great numbers.

By 2000, large areas of Europe will be under water, especially in the lowlands. As much as 50% of the landmass will be flooded, leaving Switzerland a virtual island surrounded by water.

Earth Changes Trigger

Gordon-Michael Scallion is convinced that the current bizarre weather patterns are part of the "trigger" that was setting serious Earth changes in motion. Although "El Niño" had become a scapegoat for any unsettling weather activity, Scallion stated that tectonic movement and undersea volcanic activity caused violent winds and other extreme conditions.

"When the tectonic system is stressed," he explains, "we get this release. All of this, in turn, is part of the destiny, if you will, of the Earth and the Sun."

Scallion is also concerned about another "stirring of the pot" as a result of solar earthquakes on the Sun:

> Something on the Sun induces these changes in the Earth. The kinds of things we're going to see is a major release in the Ring of Fire, perhaps multiple volcanoes going off. At any given time there are volcanoes in some stage of activity. Etna, for example, is rumbling in Italy, and there

are many other volcanoes coming to life. We're going to see this en masse!

Scallion is among those seers who expect the strong possibility of a reversal of the Earth's magnetic poles, which, some have theorized, occurs on a cyclical basis every 10,000 to 12,000 years. "The Earth doesn't flip over," he clarified. "It's a magnetic pole reversal."

The biggest changes he foresees as a result of the pole shift are weather-related:

> It will immediately change the jet stream and ground temperatures. We will literally have a new Ecosystem. Regardless of where you are on the planet, these effects are going to occur. Besides the winds and the erratic weather, these changes will be very abrupt. There will be one, then there may be a period of several weeks or months before the second and third will occur. I see these occurring within a period of about three years, between 1998 and 2001.

Volcanoes Are Escaping the "Ring of Fire"

The Earth has evolved in such a way that there are distinct regions that have tended over time to exhibit most of the volcanic and earthquake activity. These regions are collectively known as the "Ring of Fire" and include all the islands in the Pacific Ocean (e.g., Hawaii, the Philippines), and the coasts of continents which end at the Pacific (e.g., Latin America, the Western United States, including Alaska, British Columbia, the eastern coast of Russia, China, and all of Japan). If you look on a map, you will notice that these regions of the world have the highest and most rugged mountain ranges, thus you will also find the most volcanoes, active or inactive.

However, an interesting development has taken place in the last several decades of this century, even in the last few years. The world is now experiencing increased volcanic and earthquake activity in areas which have generally been considered inactive.

For example, as recently as the summer of 1996, the ancient Soufriere Hills volcano on the Caribbean island of Montserrat suddenly came to life after sitting quietly for more than a thousand years. Although it all began with a few puffs of ash, on August 21, a strong burst of steam and ash exploded from the top of the volcano, sending volcanic material nearly two miles into the air and darkening the capital city of Plymouth for thirty minutes.

In anticipation of far worse circumstances, the city began immediately to evacuate its people. Their concern was legitimate. A little over ninety years before, the Pelee volcano on the island of Martinique in the same island chain erupted, killing 20,000 people in the nearby town of St. Pierre.

Records of Magnetic Pole Reversals in Earth's Past

Professor Raymond Wheeler approaches the matter of a magnetic pole reversal and the resultant abrupt and dramatic weather changes from an entirely different perspective than that of the seers and prophets. Wheeler, who devoted himself to a study of cyclic weather patterns, suggested that profound reversals of the time and weather cycles have occurred three times in our planet's past.

During the first reversal, Wheeler claims

the vertebrate pattern emerged and stabilized sufficiently to make possible the profound modifications and differentiations of structure compelled by the more strenuous fluctuations of the Mesozoic Era.

During the second climatic optimum, another profound step in evolution occurred—the emergence of the mammal and primate patterns and the beginning of pre-human forms. Wheeler states:

The primate pattern had developed sufficiently by the end of the last ice age to permit a third profound occurrence during that series of rapid and mild fluctuations of climate. This was the emergence of modern man and his psychological and social achievements.

By the end of this century, Wheeler suggests, the deceleration-acceleration theory of the history of Earth's climate seems poised to permit a fourth profound evolutionary event: "A new and probably different series of similar general form will soon begin. Earth is about to begin a new phase of its history."

Mother Mary's Warnings for Millennium Challenges

Annie Kirkwood and her husband Byron both come from a Protestant background, so she was somewhat startled when Mother Mary began to appear to her in 1987.

"I'm not even Roman Catholic," Annie protested naively.

"Neither am I," the Blessed Mother quickly assured her, explaining that She was not the exclusive possession of any earthly religious denomination.

Although like so many millennial predictions, the warnings of Mother Mary seem severe and harsh, She told Annie that the dire forebodings could be alleviated or lessened with prayer. "Pray," She admonished Annie. "Pray for the world."

Among Mother Mary's warnings for the Millennium are the following:

- Catastrophes will move mountains, upturn seas, as new lands rise from the oceans. Some existing lands will be inundated and returned to the ocean floor.

- There will be increases in earthquakes and volcanoes, many in areas that have never before experienced such disasters.

- Quakes will greatly affect areas in Italy, Greece, Russia, Turkey, China, Columbia, and the Himalayan Mountains.

- Africa will endure eruptions from long dormant volcanoes.

- Japan will be shattered by many earthquakes.

- In the United States, the West Coast will virtually disappear.

- Weather patterns will change dramatically, with winter months colder and wetter in many areas.

- Ocean currents will change, and magnetic fields will move.

- Polar caps will melt at an increased rate. Large chunks of ice will endanger ships and seashores. The water levels of the oceans will rise, thus changing the shape of the coastlines.

- Much of China will be under mountains of ice.

- The Middle East will become cold and mountainous, but its deserts will bloom.

Following a Roadmap of Time

Whether all the grim predictions of dramatic Earth changes will actually occur by the year 2000 or 2001 remains to be seen.

Time is always a problem in examining the paranormal or in evaluating predictions. A prophet may truly see a vision of an actual event that lies ahead of us, but pinpointing the date is a real difficulty when the seer is in an altered state of consciousness in the Eternal Now. Either way, we don't have long to wait to test the accuracy of our various prophets.

Earlier in this century, Professor Raymond Wheeler and astronomer Shelby Maxwell developed accurate formulae for predicting weather cycles by investigating and recording 4,500 years of human history, rainfall patterns, tree rings, recorded sunspots, and the examination of geological strata. They foresaw a world convulsion that would occur sometime around the year 2000. In their opinion, based on their study of historical cycles, this "convulsion" would be second only to the fall of Rome and other ancient civilizations in the fifth century and the collapse of the Middle Ages in the 15th century.

Even though they warn that we face the prospect of great societal change in the coming years, they caution us to remember that each time the world has undergone a great convulsion, it has emerged better than it was before—more stable, richer, and with greater concern for human rights. Wheeler explained:

> All this confusion is the reverse side of social reconstruction. Renewed faith in democracy takes root during these times. Emancipation of the underprivileged and oppressed occurs. Men and women come into their own as free individuals. More important yet is a revival of religion and the spiritual power of whole peoples and nations.

Gordon-Michael Scallion also envisions a planetary spiritual awakening:

> A vision I've seen for 2002 is of a new Earth reborn, with its people living in harmony with each other. Lush tropical settings cover many parts of the United States. Communities seem to be located more in rural areas than in cities. The air is clean, and there no longer is an ozone hole.

Many other contemporary prophets have foreseen a coming renaissance that will involve the great masses of people participating in the economic and political structures to an extent previously unknown in history.

Those who survive the volcanoes, earthquakes, famines, floods, revolutions, and the collapse of the old world will witness a surge of renewed life force and new and viable political and economic structures.

That sounds like a positive prescription for the New Millennium.

TWELVE

GHOSTS, OUT-OF-BODY EXPERIENCES & THE HUMAN SPIRIT

While the skeptics may laugh up their sleeves at accounts of ghosts, out of body experiences, and the like, those men and women who have actually felt the eerie paranormal energy associated with hauntings very often find little in the encounter to provoke laughter.

Brad's own account of being lifted into the air by an angry ghost is enough to cast doubt in even the most skeptical of people:

They stopped using the basement in the home when Mrs. R. turned on a tap to do some washing and what appeared to be blood poured out of the faucet. About 15 years ago, a man had murdered his wife in one of the back rooms, blowing her head off with a shotgun. Strangely, grimly enough, four or five years before that gruesome murder, a similar gory slaying took place in the garage.

In addition, a man had been found stabbed to death in the basement one year when it sat empty between tenants. It had become a death house, haunted by unpleasant entities—and now a woman and her two daughters were trying to survive within its morbid walls.

As we walked down into the basement, our medium, the well-known Chicago psychic Irene Hughes caught an image of a man coming through a wall, a bearded man whose hair was long and unkempt. Mrs. R. and her older daughter paled and said that was one of the ghosts they had often seen in various rooms of the house. Irene said that the man she had seen was not the murderer of either of the two women, but another victim of terrible crimes in the house. Her impression was that he had been stabbed and had a cross carved over his heart.

Dick, a local newspaper reporter, said that such a death, along with the shotgun murders, had been attributed to the house.

While I stood in the basement murder room, my friend and unofficial bodyguard, Glenn, told me that something weird was happening with the door to the shadowy room. "You've been taking notes and been too busy to notice, but the door keeps closing on you."

I was puzzled. From the angle in which the wooden door was set, it should naturally swing open, not closed. To swing shut, the door would have to move uphill, defy gravity, and slide over a raised spot in the crude cement floor. It appeared impossible for the door to close on its own accord.

Glenn, who was also the official photographer for our psychic safaris, told me that a couple of times when he tried to take a picture of me, the door had swung nearly shut and ruined his shots. Another time, he had wedged his foot under the door to hold it, and the darn thing had nearly bent at the top because it was exerting so much pressure against his shoe.

"All right," I shrugged. "If it wants to be closed so badly, now that I've finished with my notes, close and lock it!" I watched Glenn swing the door to the jamb, then saw that he actually had to lift it in order to make a tight fit. The troublesome basement door finally closed and locked, we moved on to join the others.

A few minutes later, as we gathered in an upstairs room, Irene said she was experiencing a strange, electrical feeling, as if something were moving underneath her. Mrs. R. and others began to express the same sensation. Then two or three of us felt a force rushing against them.

Bam! Bam! Bam! Three loud explosions sounded from the basement. I had an image of the locked door of the darkened murder room swinging open, releasing an angry, powerful, ghostly force. The same unseen force that was moving under us, lifting each of us, seven in all, several inches into the air. We were only levitated for a moment, but it was a moment none of us would ever forget.

When Glenn and Dick ran down the basement stairs to investigate, they found the locked door to the basement death room standing wide open. There was no way that we could tame whatever was in that room, whatever evil that had possessed the house, quite that easily.

There are dozens and dozens of folks out there who are convinced that they have come face-to-eerie-face with a ghost. And among those ghostly accounts there are also some very interesting photographs of otherworldly entities.

One interesting picture came from a man in Arizona. A stone mason had been doing some remodeling work in an old house and wanted a record of his work for his portfolio. But when he got the photo back from the lab, the man could clearly see a white, cloudy outline of some being hovering in the room where the stone mason had done his work. We believe this being was a ghost. Ghosts are spirit beings—probably spirits of the dead—that are somehow trapped here on Earth, though we have no idea why.

More Americans Believe in Ghosts than Ever Before

Numerous national polls provide additional documentation of a haunted reality for millions of Americans.

For example, the "USA Snapshots" feature in the April 20, 1998 issue of *USA TODAY* states that a general belief in the "Beyond" has grown considerably since the 1970s. In a poll taken in 1976, only 12% of adults said that they believed in the possibility of encounters with spirits of the dead achieved through mediums or haunting phenomena. In 1998, according to the recent poll, 52% of adult Americans believe in spirit contact.

The December 1996 issue of *George*, a monthly magazine of political commentary, contained a survey to determine what Americans believed about a number of spiritual/religious/paranormal subjects. The survey revealed that 39% of people believed in ghosts and haunted houses.

In 1994, Jeffrey S. Levin, an associate professor at Eastern Virginia Medical School, Norfolk, Virginia, carefully analyzed a national sociological survey conducted by the National Opinion Research Center, University of Chicago. He found that two-thirds of Americans stated that they had undergone at least one "mystical experience." Of that astonishingly high figure, 39.9% claimed that they had an encounter with a ghost or had achieved contact with the spirit of a deceased person.

In the Steiger questionnaire of Mystical, Paranormal, and UFO Experiences, the survey process accumulated data indicating that among Steiger readers or lecture attendees, 48% are convinced that they have seen a ghost. Interestingly, 42% have perceived the spirit of a departed one and 61% claim that they have encountered spirit entities in haunted places.

Classifying Ghosts and Apparitions

Psychical researchers have long recognized four main classifications of ghost and apparitions:

- Ghosts or apparitions which habitually appear in a room, house, or locale. A general rule of thumb indicates that ghosts are strangers to the observers while apparitions are images of people who are known to the observer.

- Crisis-apparitions in which a recognized apparition is seen, heard, or felt when the individual represented by the image is undergoing a crisis, especially death. A classic illustration would be that of the son who is preparing for bed in his home in New Jersey who looks up to see his father, a mechanic in Texas, standing in the doorway, raising his arm in farewell. A few moments later, the man's mother calls from Texas to say the father has just passed away.

- Post-mortem apparitions in which a recognized apparition is seen or heard long after the person represented by the ethereal image has died.

- Experimental cases in out-of-body experience, astral projection, in which an agent has deliberately attempted to make his spirit form appear to a particular participant.

We might also add to the above classifications the following addenda:

- *Phantoms*: Ghostly apparitions that have been seen by so many people over so many years that the images have literally begun to take on independent existences of their own, thus becoming "psychic marionettes," responding to the fears and expectations of their human audiences. Nearly every community has its traditional phantom, such as a Phantom Nun that haunts the ruins of a convent, a Phantom Horseman that guards an old bridge, a Phantom Hound that stands watch over a long-deceased master's gravestone.

- *Poltergeists*: The poltergeist (German for pelting, throwing, ghost) may not really be a ghost at all, but the psychokinetic disturbances caused by a living human (usually an adolescent or someone undergoing the stresses of severe psychological adjustment). Unconscious aggression toward others is manifested when the psychic energy overturns furniture, smashes dinner plates, and shatters windows. Perhaps the most disruptive and unsettling kind of hauntings are those in which the poltergeistic psyche of a human interacts with a ghostly manifestation which may already exist in a home. When that occurs, the psychical investigator must be prepared to deal with a cosmic carnival of terror.

Psychical Society Begins Hunting Ghosts in 1882

In 1882, the first major undertaking of the newly formed British Society for Psychical Research was to conduct a survey that asked one main question. What percentage of people had ever, "while completely awake," had a vivid impression of seeing, hearing, or being touched by a ghost or apparition "which impression, so far as you could discover, was not due to any external physical cause?" Of the 17,000 people surveyed, 1,684 answered, "yes," and those individuals were sent additional forms requesting more details of the experience.

The committee was eventually able to conclude that although apparitions are connected with certain events other than death, they are more likely to be linked with the death of individuals than with anything else. They also learned that visual manifestations were more common by far than auditory experiences. Of the 1,087 visual cases reported, 283 had been shared by more than one observer. Those who answered the second form indicated that they had not been ill when they had witnessed their manifestations and insisted that the images were quite unlike the bizarre, nightmarish entities that might appear during high fevers or high consumption of alcohol.

Of the 493 respondents who reported auditory manifestations, 94 had occurred when another person had been present. Therefore, about one-third of the cases had been collective, that is, experienced by more than one person at a time.

After the findings of the Society were made public, their offices began to be flooded by personal accounts of spontaneous cases of ghosts and apparitions. In order to aid an appointed committee in the handling of such an influx of material, the Society for Psychical Research worked out a series of questions that could be applied to each case. Over 100 years later, their list still serves as a useful guide for investigators:

1. Is the account firsthand?

2. Was it written or told before the corresponding event was known?

3. Has the principal witness been corroborated?

4. Was the percipient awake at the time?

5. Was the percipient an educated person of good character?

6. Was the apparition recognized?

7. Was it seen out of doors?

8. Was the percipient anxious or in a state of expectancy?

9. Could relevant details have been read back into the narrative after the event?

10. Could the coincidence between the experience and the event be accounted for by chance?

What Makes a Ghost?

G.N.M. Tyrrell saw the ghost or apparition as a "psychological marionette" which is projected by an individual in a time of crisis or great emotion. To Tyrrell, the mechanism of a haunting was similar to an idea, and, at the same time, very much like a pattern. Thus the "idea-pattern" finds sensory expression in the apparition, which has been produced by the dramatic idea of a human psyche.

Tyrrell's "idea-pattern" is distinguished by three general characteristics: It is *dynamic*, for it is usually associated with an initiating drive, and *creative*, for it manifests an urge toward expression and completeness. Finally, it is *teleological*, for it is marvelously resourceful in adaptation in adjusting means to ends.

Edmund Gurney theorized that the collective sighting of a ghost is due to a sort of telepathic "infection." One person sees the phantom and in turn, telepathically, influences another person, and so on.

Harry Price developed the "psychic ether" theory of hauntings in which he hypothesized that a certain level of mind may create a mental image that has a degree of persistence in the psychic ether. This mental image may also contain a telepathic ability by which it can affect other minds.

The collective emotions and thought images of a person who has lived in a house for some time may have intensely "charged" the psychic ether of the place. This is especially relevant if there were powerful emotions, such as those of intense hatred, fear, or sorrow—or if they had been supercharged by an act of violence. In Price's theory, the original agent—the human inhabitant of the house—has no direct part in the haunting. It is the charged psychic ether which, when presented with a suitable mind of the proper telepathic affinity, co-operates in the production of the idea-pattern of a ghost.

It can be said that every old house, courtroom, hospital, castle, railroad depot is "haunted." Any long-inhabited place, which has served as a container of human activity, almost certainly bears existing memory traces. Just the same, a multitude of mental images may over-saturate the majority of old homes and public places and leave only a mass of impressions that create the peculiar "atmosphere" that so many rooms and locales have. It is only when an idea-pattern that has been charged with enormous psychic intensity finds the mental level of an observer who has the proper quality of telepathic affinity that a ghost can appear.

Dissolving the Barriers Between Worlds

What if all the barriers between the worlds were suddenly removed? What if contact between the two worlds—one of spirits, the other of physical humans—just came tumbling down? What would that mean for all of us on the physical plane?

Presumably, we would all become more spiritual beings here on Earth. We would have to recognize the Oneness of all things.

More and more individuals are recognizing that the barriers between the seen and unseen worlds have always been very transparent. The Beyond has always been quite accessible. What barriers do exist, are largely of our own making, caused by our materialism, our personal prejudices, and, yes, our unwillingness to set aside human ego and accept the gifts of Spirit.

Perhaps nothing demonstrates the fragile nature of the barrier between worlds more than the near-death experience (NDE). With the advent of advanced medical technology, more men, women, and children are undergoing NDEs and returning to life than ever before in human history. Thus, many individuals have the unique transient experience of becoming a temporary ghost, sometimes even visiting ethereal regions in the afterlife, before returning to life in a physical body. And thousands of people who had not previously believed or understood that they were multidimensional beings composed of spirit and flesh are undergoing dramatic transformations of character.

Dr. Moody Explores *Life After Life*

Dr. Raymond Moody, who is both a medical doctor and the holder of a doctorate degree in philosophy, has interviewed thousands of patients who returned to their bodies after a NDE and who were revived and returned to life through medical treatment. In such works as his *Life After Life*, Dr. Moody has found many common traits among these experiences.

Survivors have the sensation of moving rapidly through a long, dark tunnel before "popping" outside of their physical bodies. If they were in hospital rooms or other enclosures, they often remembered floating near the ceiling and watching the medical teams attempting to revive their physical bodies. Many NDE survivors have also reported seeing their life literally flashing before their eyes. They are often welcomed to the other world by previously deceased friends or relatives.

Whether or not they are of a religious background, they often report an encounter with a brilliant, intense white light that may assume the form of an angel, a guide, a teacher, Father Abraham, or a Christ-figure.

The Research of Dr. Bruce Goldberg

Dr. Bruce Goldberg has hypnotized thousands of patients in a meticulous examination of the near-death experience. His pattern profile of the near-death survivor is quite similar in many respects to Dr. Moody's cases.

The survivor moves down what appears to be a tunnel toward a white light. At first there may be some confusion as to what is happening and some frustration at being unable to gain the attention of the living.

Survivors describe being met by deceased friends and relatives, as well as an encounter with an angel, a guide, or a spirit being who arrives to comfort and to instruct.

Depending on the length of the experience, the survivors may find themselves in a beautiful paradise. Before they return to physical life, they discover that their consciousness has expanded far beyond that which it was during their mortal existence. In fact, because of this expanded consciousness and sense of "paradise," many survivors experience an unwillingness to leave the postmortem state and return to their physical bodies.

Other Surveys of Near-Death Survivors

In his *Life at Death*, Kenneth Ring released the results of data that he had complied from 102 men and women who had undergone NDEs. In his tabulations, Ring reported that:

- 60% of the survivors found that their NDE had brought them a sense of peace;

- 37% reported a separation of consciousness from the physical body;

- 23% mentioned the process of entering a dark tunnel;

- 16% said that they had encountered the brilliant light; and

- 10% claimed that they had entered the light.

The Steiger Questionnaire disclosed that:

- 76% of the respondents claimed that their soul left the physical body during an accident, a serious illness, a surgical procedure, or some other kind of NDE;

- 57% said that they visited a heavenly realm or dimension during their NDE;

- 60% reported that they received an inspirational message from a Higher Intelligence during their experience;

- 74% report regular out-of-body experiences; and

- 72% claim an illumination experience while out of the body.

The evidence continues to pile up. A recent Gallup Poll stated that 15% of all Americans claim to have had a near-death experience. A survey conducted in 1991 by Dr. Colin Ross, associate professor of psychiatry at the University of Manitoba in Winnipeg, suggests that as many as one in three people have left their physical bodies and returned—most often during times of crisis, extreme pain, and near-death.

Dannion Brinkley Undergoes Spiritual Transformation

Struck by lightning in 1975, Dannion Brinkley, author of *Saved by the Light,* said that he somehow watched medics working on him from a point somewhere above his physical body. In what was measured as 28 minutes of Earth time, Brinkley "died" and traveled in another dimension in order to receive profound revelations that completely transformed his life. Dr. Raymond Moody later termed Dannion's journey the most amazing and complete near-death experience that he had encountered after researching 20,000 such accounts.

After he had traveled through a dark tunnel, a spirit joined Dannion Brinkley and led him to a crystal city, awash with light and peace. As if they were wingless birds, he and the angelic entity entered a "city of cathedrals"

> made entirely of a crystal substance that glowed with a light that shone powerfully from within. We stood before one. I felt small and insignificant next to this architectural masterpiece. Clearly this was built by angels to show the grandeur of God.... The walls were made of large glass rocks that glowed with a life inside them. These structures were not about specific religions of any kind. They were there as a monument to the glory of God.

The once rowdy and reckless Dannion Brinkley was admonished by his angelic instructors that when he returned to the "earth plane," he was to use his new psychic and spiritual gifts to aid the dying and the desperate. He was told that human beings were really powerful spiritual beings intended to create good on Earth. Such good was not usually accompanied by bold actions, "but in singular acts of kindness between people."

Wise and kindly beings of light presented him with visions of dramatic future events that would come to pass on Earth. When Brinkley returned to consciousness and life, he wrote down 117 of these occurrences. In the ensuing years, 95 of them had taken place.

The possibility of an afterlife holds a fascination like no other subject. We believe that a person has a soul, and we will continue to search for evidence about exactly what happens after this life.

Sherry Steiger Visits Crystal City Deep in Meditation

Brad's wife, Sherry, has had two near-death experiences: the first while a child suffering from rheumatic fever, the second as an adult when she ran a near-fatal fever during a kidney infection. But it was during an out of body experience while she was in an extremely deep state of meditation for *nearly five hours* that she visited a heavenly crystal city such as the one described by Dannion Brinkley during his NDE after being struck by lightning.

After praying and relaxing, she remembers leaving her body in a sudden "poof" and being escorted by a Light Being through the "most mystically beautiful experience of my life." She described the event:

> The Light Being, a facet of the Divine Force, was so loving and caring and showed me so many things. The Being did not seem to have a gender, but I felt as though I knew him/her. It seemed

as though we traveled through galaxies, making stops along the way. There was one place—maybe it was a planet...maybe it was the New Jerusalem—where the beauty was far above anything I've ever dreamed possible. It was like a crystal/diamond planet, reflecting and refracting the purest, most brilliant colors. The light all around was effervescent.

As a "living crystal," I became fused with the light. I became the Light! Blissful elation permeated every cell of my being. How I wished that others might be able to experience this powerful love...this perfect love....I was told that I would remember only a small part of what I had seen. More would be revealed to my conscious mind as I shared and used the experience to help others...

...I know there is an absolute reality...a life beyond...a continuation of life...a perfect, all-encompassing power of love and peace, order and law. This absolute reality is the love we are to be...it's the love we were...it's the love we are.

The Most Extraordinary Achievement of Human Will

Numerous researchers have demonstrated that such phenomena as out-of-body experiences are natural processes and are an essential part of what it is to be human. In fact, as Frederic W.H. Myers, an esteemed pioneer research of psychic phenomena, put it, OBE may be the most extraordinary achievement of the human will:

What can lie further outside any known capacity than the power to cause a semblance of oneself to appear at a distance? What can be more a central action—more manifestly the outcome of whatsoever is deepest and most unitary in a man's whole being? Of all vital phenomena, I say this is the most significant; this self-projection is the one definite act that it seems as though a man might perform equally well before and after bodily death.

Creating Our Afterlife While on Earth

H.H. Price, a former president of the British Society for Psychical Research, once put forth the view that the whole point of our life on Earth might very well be to provide us with a stockpile of memories. Out of these memories we might construct a meaningful image world at the time of our death. Such a world would be a psychological world and not a physical one, even though it would seem to be quite physical to those who would experience it.

In Price's hypothesis, the Other World would be the manifestation in image form of the memories and desires of its inhabitants, including their repressed or unconscious memories and desires. Indeed, this afterlife, this "Heaven," might be every bit as detailed, as vivid, and complex as the present perceptible world that we experience as living physical entities.

Price also conceptualized that the inhabitants of their individual "image-worlds" might very well maintain a vivid and persistent image of the physical body they once occupied while on Earth. He explained:

The surviving personality, according to this concept of survival, is in actual fact an immaterial
entity. But if one habitually thinks of oneself as
embodied (as well one might, at least for a considerable time), an image of one's own body might
be, as it were, the persistent center of one's image
world, much as the perceived physical body is the
persistent center of one's perceptible world in this
present life.

Auras: Physical Manifestations of the Soul

Mark Smith believes that auras are the physical
manifestation of the soul, and that our immediate likes
and dislikes of people are very often based upon our
innate psychic ability to perceive the band of colored
light that emanates from their bodies.

The perception of auras is not strictly a matter of
psychic ability. The aura can be measured by conventional physics in such techniques as those employed in
Kirlian photography. According to Smith, "there's an
energy field outside of the human body, not touching
the body...and it's been measured from .05 volts...up to
80 volts for two or three seconds at a time."

Smith, author of *Auras: See Them in Only 60 Seconds*, was a professional musician in the mid-to-late
70s, opening for such rock groups as the Grateful Dead
Jefferson Starship. And he claims that it was the late
Jerry Garcia of the Grateful Dead that first showed him
how to see peoples' auras.

Smith provided a simplified step-by-step version of
how anyone might obtain meaningful glimpses of the
human aura. The simplest method of all, Smith said,

may be to employ "focal length change," the method one uses to see objects hidden within computer art:

1. Stand the person against a white or off-white colored wall. Try to use indirect lighting if possible.

2. Stand at least 10 feet away from the subject.

3. The subject should sway slightly from side to side and breathe deeply.

4. Look beyond the person's shoulder and try to focus on the wall, remembering the analogy to the computer art method.

5. You should eventually see a narrow white band around the subject's body. This is the etheric aura.

6. It may take some time [it took Mark Smith three days], but eventually you should begin to see some color. This is called the astral aura.

Freeing the Spirit During Lucid Dreaming

Over the years, such researchers as Patricia Garfield, J. Timothy Green, and Stephen La Berge have suggested the process of lucid dreaming as a means of allowing the spirit to travel free of the physical body. "Lucid dreams," Green explained, "are quite simply those dreams in which the dreamer becomes conscious while dreaming that he or she is, in fact, dreaming."

As Green and other researchers of altered states of consciousness have determined, it is possible to think logically while, at the same time, being quite aware that the body is sleeping. Green claims that he learned how to practice lucid dreaming in three months and is convinced that any one who makes a concerted effort to achieve the lucid dream state can also accomplish OBEs without the slightest danger to his or her well being.

In his *Lucid Dreaming*, LaBerge states that fully lucid dreamers realize that the persons they appear to be in the dream scenario and not who they actually are. Once they no longer identify with their egos, they are free to alter the dream in order to allow the content and action to become a transcendental process. Not only may one therefore achieve OBEs, but also eliminate certain fears, problems, and misconceptions from their lives.

Patricia Garfield, author of *Creative Dreaming*, maintains that practically anything one might wish to happen may occur in lucid dreams. Her research indicates that such dream states are achieved more easily after several hours of sleep. She also advises dreamers not to allow themselves to become too emotional or they will tend to awaken.

LaBerge suggests that those attempting successful lucid dreams ask themselves immediately upon awaking whether or not they were dreaming. He also recommends asking oneself frequently through the waking day, "Am I dreaming now?" Such systematic queries will encourage the habit of asking that question while one is actually in the dream state.

Green and LaBerge agree that the power of intent is very significant in achieving lucid dreams. One should declare the intention of having a lucid dream several times during the waking hours and repeat the intent before falling asleep. "Lucid dreaming rarely occurs without our intending it," LaBerge said, "which means having the mental set to recognize when we are dreaming; thus, intention forms a part of any deliberate effort to induce dreams."

Whether one attains an out-of-body experience through the practice of lucid dreaming, meditation, illumination, astral projection or any other type of individual mystical experience, the rewards to be gained are many and highly significant for one's continued quest on the "earth plane." These benefits include the development of deeper qualities of understanding, a diminished concern for the selfish interests of the world; a powerful sense of wholeness and of Oneness with the cosmos; increased vitality and an improvement in physical health; and a much greater patience to fulfill your true mission in life.

THIRTEEN

MIND TRAVEL THROUGH
TIME & SPACE

We don't always have to search for visitors from
other worlds to find extraordinary powers. Humans
possess their own innate powers. Theoretically, each
person can project the mind/soul self, glimpse the future, view the past, and communicate telepathically.
Theoretically, each of us has the capability to visit other
dimensions, to become aware of other worlds of reality
and to perceive the universe as it really is, thus defin-
ing our true place within its limitless boundaries.

Most of these talents fall into the category of extrasensory perception (ESP), which has long been defined
as the acquisition by human or animal mind of information which it could not have received by normal,
sensory means. However, there are researchers who say
such talents are not "extra" sensory at all, but true, al-

beit sometimes slumbering, aspects of the normal mind.

Other researchers argue that the phenomena cannot really be called "perception," because the receiver of such information doesn't always know if the knowledge is right or wrong when he or she first perceives it. It takes a corroborating incident to convince anyone that he or she has perceived anything through "extrasensory" means.

Therefore, many researchers prefer to term such phenomena as "paranormal cognition," but this label is subject to the same sort of criticism as "perception." In addition, many of those who research such powers of mind insist that the material in their field will eventually merge with present day physics, so the very adjective "paranormal" may be considered a misnomer.

To avoid such criticisms, current parascientific research prefers to include all of the individual classifications of the unexplained (precognition, clairvoyance, telepathy, poltergeists, ghosts) and all related phenomena under the term "Psi," from the Greek *psyche*, designating the human soul, mind, or spirit.

Most People Repress Their Natural Psychic Abilities

Numerous experiments and countless hours of laboratory research have demonstrated that as children many of us utilize our Psi abilities to a considerable degree, but as we mature, we tend to inhibit these faculties of mind or allow them to atrophy. A general consensus of Psi researchers contends most people completely repress these abilities in favor of normal means of perception.

Many parapsychologists, anthropologists, and psychologists as early as Sigmund Freud, have theorized that these Psi faculties may have been the original methods by which our early ancestors understood one another. As a better means of communication evolved, one that could readily be intelligible to the sensory organs, the original archaic methods were pushed into the background of the human subconscious where they still persist, waiting to manifest themselves under certain conditions.

It is obvious to all serious investigators of the unexplained that some individuals, functioning largely according to their moods and psychic needs, are able to draw upon their Psi abilities. And some talented individuals are able to make regular and practical use of the seemingly rare powers of Psi.

Remote Viewing Seeks to Make Practical Use of Psi

If you are like most people, you've wondered on occasion what another person was really thinking. Well, some people know. They have developed clairvoyance and telepathic abilities through certain meditative techniques. Indeed, there are some people who have developed these abilities to such a high level that the Russian and U.S. governments have become interested. In their attempt to justify research funds, perhaps, and to add credibility to their work, these people call this "scientific remote viewing."

Remote viewing claims of such individuals as Ed Dames, Lyn Buchanan, Joe McMoneagle, and Paul Smith have becoming increasingly popularized.

It surprises a lot of people to learn that particularly during the 1970s and 80s, the CIA funded research at

Stanford Research Institute in the area of remote viewing. Remote viewers have 'seen' a variety of things,
many in relation to national security interests, and
have been tested for, and produced, a high accuracy
rate.

Of course, remote viewing works because these people are actually transporting themselves spiritually to
some remote location to investigate what is called their
"target." For many years now, this spiritual "transpor-
tation" has been called astral projection or out-of-body
experience, but remote viewers prefer to term this old
metaphysical practice as a kind of mental technology.

Identifying the Facets of Psi Abilities

Psi activity is subdivided into many types:

- *Precognition* is that facility of mind whereby the person seems to receive a glimpse of the future and
  gains knowledge of events yet to occur.

- *Telepathy* is the transference of thought from one
  mind to another. Distance and time seem unable to
  affect this Psi phenomenon. Tests have been conducted around the world—and even from Earth to
  the Moon.

- *Clairvoyance* is the awareness, without physical aids
  or normal sensory means, of what is going on elsewhere.

- *Psychokinesis* and/or telekinesis is the direct action
  of mind on matter. This movement of objects caused
  by some force unknown to physical science is the

parapsychologists' nominee as the culprit involved in poltergeist cases—those bizarre occurrences when bottles and crockery become airborne, fires break out on living room tables, and disembodied voices cackle from unseen sources.

• *Out-of-Body Experience* and/or *Astral Projection* are the projection of the mind-spirit-soul from its fleshly domicile.

• *Psychometry* is the determination of facts about an object's owner simply from contact with object, such as an old ring, bracelet, necklace, and so forth.

Of course, each of these types of phenomena may be a single manifestation of the same energy, force, or function of the mind-spirit-soul.

Psi Works Best During Altered States of Consciousness

Many Psi activities occur while one is either asleep or in some altered state of consciousness, such as trance or hypnosis. This would seem to indicate even more profoundly that each of us, in our subconscious, has the faculties necessary to focus on our Psi abilities. In the literature of psychical research, many clairvoyant and precognitive experiences have been found to have taken place in dreams or while the person was in a relaxed state of mind.

Those people who easily remember their dreams have firsthand proof that there are various levels of mind. One level authors the "script" for the evening's performance, another level directs the "play" with its various scenarios and cloaks them with symbolic meaning, and yet another level acts as the anticipatory audience for the performance.

Some years ago, Dr. Jan Ehrenwald theorized that telepathy appeared to work best when either the agent (sender) or percipient (receiver) was in a state of "psychological inadequacy." In his opinion, telepathic communications are most effective when the conscious mind is groggy with sleep, befogged by hypnosis, trance, fever, or physical exhaustion.

Difficult to Generate Psi Phenomena in a Laboratory

The difficulty that so many conventional scientists have in accepting the unexplained regions of Psi phenomena is that accounts of clairvoyance, telepathy, and apparitions are largely anecdotal. They seldom fit into the requirements demanded of all conventional sciences: 1] that such phenomena may be produced by controlled and repeatable experiments; 2] that such phenomena may be placed in a hypothesis comprehensive enough to include all Psi activity—from telepathy to poltergeists, from water dowsing to precognition.

The enormous difficulty in fulfilling such requirements can be immediately grasped by anyone with the slightest knowledge of Psi phenomena and the process by which they work. It would be impossible, for example, to repeat the apparition of a man's father as it appeared to him at the moment of his death. This phenomenon, called a "crisis apparition," occurs only at death and the man's father cannot die again under laboratory conditions.

Psi phenomena tend to be almost completely spontaneous in nature, and ungovernable elements of mood and emotion play enormously important roles in any type of experience currently labeled "unexplained." As many serious researchers have noted, people who experience Psi phenomena are seldom aware of a telepathic, clairvoyant, or precognitive process at work within them. They are only really aware of the *product* of that process. In fact, it seems readily apparent from laboratory experiments that exceedingly *conscious* efforts to determine any Psi process at work within an individual will either completely destroy the process or greatly diminish its effectiveness.

Therefore, laboratory experiments have sometimes established, by incredibly laborious tests and a veritable mountain of statistics, only slightly better than chance evidence of the validity of telepathy, clairvoyance, precognition, and psychokinesis. No one has yet managed to reproduce an apparition in a laboratory, and it is remarkable that a gifted psychic, such as the late Olof Jonsson, who consistently "guessed" 100 out of 100 cards correctly, could retain enough energy to have survived an endless series of card-guessing experiments.

As we have noted, Psi phenomena depend upon emotion and spontaneity to be most effective. And what is more sterile and emotionless than a laboratory? And what would serve to stifle spontaneity more than a series of exceedingly boring and repetitive card or dice guessing experiments?

To bring Psi phenomena into the laboratory is to inhibit the spontaneous features of the phenomena in order to attempt to maintain control over its normal functioning. This is like bringing an African lion into a zoo in order to study its behavior in its natural environment.

Pioneer Remote Viewing at Stanford Research Institute

Beginning in 1972, our friends and colleagues at Stanford Research Institute (SRI) were able to demonstrate the validity of Psi phenomena so effectively that NASA, the Air Force, the CIA, and the Navy funded their research to the sum of a million dollars a year for the next 20 years. Top researchers Harold Puthoff and Russell Targ assembled such experienced psychics as Ingo Swann, Hella Hammid, and Pat Price for some of the early experiments, and the results produced by the mind travelers astounded the intelligence community.

Ingo Swann, an artist from New York, was given a set of geographical coordinates by the CIA and asked to describe what he was able to perceive at each site. Swann was provided the coordinates for the miniscule Antarctic island of Kerguelen, where the French maintained a research base. Swann, who had no prior knowledge of the installation or any familiarity with the area, was able to "view" the location so precisely that he proceeded to draw a detailed map. His sketch depicted an airstrip, two white cylindrical tanks, parked trucks, a radar antenna and other details of the base. Later, a French scientist who had served in the Antarctic installation found Swann's sketch so precise that he found it difficult to believe that the psychic had not actually been there.

Swann commented to journalist Paul Bannister that he had simply utilized his mind to "...travel half a world away to an unknown location while leaving my body sitting comfortably on a sofa at Stanford."

Sometime in 1983, Swann, under the direction of Dr. Harold Puthoff, appeared to have achieved a breakthrough in remote viewing. He felt that he had developed an accurate model of how the collective unconscious communicated the target information to the conscious awareness of the psychics. Swann further believed that Psi abilities, such as remote viewing, were innate faculties accessible to all who would discipline themselves to be effective. The model he formulated appeared capable of establishing a rigid set of instructions and guiding any dedicated potential remote viewer to a high degree of accuracy in collecting target information.

Former Burbank Police Commissioner Pat Price was given the map coordinates of a Soviet nuclear facility in central Asia where a high-energy beam weapon was being developed to disable U.S. space satellites or missiles.

Targ told Bannister that he remembers Price sitting in the lab at Stanford and sending his mind to the coordinates he had been given and describing what he saw. The psychic viewer was able to perceive "a huge crane; a two-legged gantry (movable structure used to move a crane) on a railroad line, and smooth spheres, 60 feet in diameter."

When a U.S. spy satellite took high-resolution photographs of the area, CIA operatives clearly saw the crane, the gantry on its railroad, and other equipment that Price had revealed through his Psi abilities. Targ emphasizes that no one in U.S. intelligence had been aware of the equipment placement in that location before the psychic had "seen" it from his seat in the Stanford lab. What is more, Price had described "equipment inside the closely guarded site where the spy satellites couldn't see," Targ said. "Three years later, on-ground spies confirmed Price's reports."

A number of the early participants in the Stanford Research Insitute's program had been previously connected with L. Ron Hubbard's Scientology. Ingo Swann made no secret of his association with Scientology and has even attributed his success to techniques that he learned while studying the various courses.

Ed Dames and Technical Remote Viewing

As increasing millions were granted to SRI, the military stepped in more fully to manage the projects. Major Ed Dames and General Stubblebine were two such managers. Stubblebine directed SRI, and later broadened the activities to include Tarot card reading and the New Age practice of channeling.

Ed Dames left government service some years ago and devoted himself to establishing Technical Remote Viewing as a private enterprise. He has explained how he wished to develop a method of turning psychic viewing into a discipline with a much higher degree of reliability. His research progressed to the point where he developed Technical Remote Viewing (TRV), a method which eliminates human consciousness from the problem under consideration and taps the collective unconscious in a disciplined way.

Dames stresses that Technical Remote Viewing is not to be confused with such Psi phenomena as clairvoyance or precognition. TRV takes a more disciplined approach and pursues specific answers to specific problems, thereby achieving "target lock-on" at specific times and on demand. The target of TRV may be any person, event, or episode in the present, past, or future.

Explaining the process, Dames calls TRV a structured, highly disciplined technique that downloads very accurate and detailed information from the collective unconscious. It actually employs a process by which the unconscious mind communicates with conscious awareness. In the view of Ed Dames, the collective un-conscious is like a huge library: "We call that the ma-trix. Remote viewers search the matrix, or data base, controlling the search by looking for specific things, not 'just anything.'"

In contrast, Dames maintains, precognitive dreams, out-of-body experiences, or clairvoyant impressions may still be infiltrated by the imagination, thus cloud-ing the data received through these paranormal sources. By perfecting the TRV techniques, Dames and his PsiTech team of the top 50 remote viewers can offer their clients 100% accuracy.

After the crash of TWA Flight 800 on July 17, 1996, PsiTech undertook the task of viewing what had hap-pened to the ill-fated Boeing 747. A team of eight re-mote viewers soon discovered that the cause of the crash had not been a missile, the result of sabotage, or the product of negligence. They perceived that a bro-ken part on a hydraulic pump on the inboard Number Three engine had fractured the engine housing, thereby breaking up into pieces of shrapnel which, in turn, ruptured a fuel tank. Dripping fuel, mixing with air, caused a fuel-air "mist" that exploded and severed the right wing of the aircraft.

Responding to the general public's anxiety toward the future, Dames comments that although the future is "fuzzy" and "reality is malleable," there seems no way to avoid the catastrophic ecological events that lie ahead for all of humanity. The Earth changes to come will be grim and will occur over the next few years. However, Dames believes that the ultimate outcome of these natural disasters will be positive and that the Earth will enjoy better times by about the year 2020.

When asked to view the enigma of extraterrestrial visitors in the past, present, and future of Earth, Dames' perceptions included:

- Those beings popularly called the Grays are an ancient race of extraterrestrials who are hundreds of millions of evolutionary years ahead of humankind.

- The Grays have interacted with *Homo sapiens* throughout history, sometimes even caring for developing humanity. For instance, Dames believes that the "ant people" who nurtured the Hopi in their ancient history were actually the Grays.

- When Mars began losing those elements in its atmosphere that support life, the Grays rescued a segment of the Martian population and transported them to Earth. Because of the vast difference in atmospheres, the Martians could neither reproduce nor survive on this planet until, over the centuries, the Grays were able to re-engineer the Martian genetic stock.

Remote viewing undoubtedly has the promise of amazing breakthroughs in its future. In the meantime, however, since the general public is not privy to the techniques refined by Dames for his Technical Remote viewers, we will continue to pursue the more traditional approaches to developing clairvoyance and the other Psi abilities.

Experiments in "Traveling Clairvoyance" circa 1849

In 1849, the famous English mathematician, Augustus De Morgan wrote of his first experience with what came to be known as "traveling clairvoyance." The early mesmerists (hypnotists) conducted many experiments during which subjects would be asked to "go somewhere" mentally and describe what they saw, and some truly astonishing reports came out of these early tests.

In the particular experiment of which De Morgan wrote, he told of dining at a friend's house about a mile from his own. De Morgan's wife was not present, having remained at home to treat a young epileptic girl with mesmeric therapy. When De Morgan returned home, his wife greeted him with the words: "We have been after you."

While in a hypnotic trance, the girl, whose clairvoyant abilities had been demonstrated on numerous previous occasions, had been instructed by Mrs. De Morgan to "follow" Mr. De Morgan to his friend's home.

When the young woman's mother heard the name of the street on which De Morgan could be located, she said that she could never find her way there. She had never been so far away from Camden Town.

However, the subject was undaunted by the assignment to follow Mr. De Morgan. In a moment, she announced that she stood before the house. Mrs. De Morgan told her that she must enter the house. The subject replied that she could not pass through the door until she had entered the gate. Mrs. De Morgan bade her subject to continue to simulate entering first the gate, then the door to the house, and continue to locate Mr. De Morgan.

Mrs. De Morgan was puzzled by the requirement of entering a gate before the door, and it was only upon her husband's return that the mystery was explained. Since she had never been at this particular person's home, Mrs. De Morgan was not aware that the house stood in a garden and that the front gate was reached only after one had entered at the garden gate.

Once the girl said that she was inside the house, she indicated that she could hear voices upstairs. She "walked" up the stairs and provided a detailed description of the people, the furniture in the room, pictures, objects of art, and the colors of the drapes.

When Mr. De Morgan studied his wife's notes of the experiment, he was admittedly awed by the clairvoyantly acquired information, and he verified that each detail was precise and exact. He was even more astonished when the girl described the dinner menu and repeated the conversations that she had overhead while observing the group in her spirit essence.

Mind-Traveling Live on Television

Beginning in the summer of 1968, Brad participated in a number of experiments in traveling clairvoyance, or what is called "mind travel." They began with target locations within a few miles of Brad's office in Iowa and eventually achieved great success with hits as far away as Chicago, Long Island, and Great Britain.

Their best subject was a friend named Reva Smock. Reva was a twin, and she and her sister had a strong telepathic and clairvoyant linkup, which had intensified as they had matured. Under light trance states, Reva was also proficient at medical diagnosis at great distances and of "shining the healing light" on individuals who were present in Brad's office. A number of dramatic healings were accomplished, one of which was written up in a medical journal.

The "moment of truth" for their research came when they were challenged to demonstrate mind traveling on a live television program telecast from an ABC affiliate in Chicago:

> First we were asked to send Reva into a scene from the past. We had conducted a few such experiments, but without a great deal of enthusiasm because how could anyone really verify a true hit? You can say you traveled back in time to watch Columbus discover America, but how could you prove it?
>
> What the producer Merrill Mazeur and the host Paul Benzaquin had done was arrange for a Lincoln scholar and specialist on Gettysburg to be present for our appearance, so that our challenge would be to send Reva back in time to the day when Lincoln gave the famous Gettysburg Address. Interestingly, after her post-hypnotic suggestion, Reva traveled back to the correct moment in time and saw Lincoln give his speech through the eyes of a young girl who was standing near the front of the crowd. She then proceeded to describe certain movements on the part of Lincoln that enabled the historian to state that she had described the event to his satisfaction.
>
> Perhaps no one could prove that Reva went back in time, but a respected university historian testified that she described a number of actions by Lincoln that would only have been known to a specialist, such as himself.
>
> The next test was more demanding. We were challenged to send Reva to Benzaquin's home in Boston and to describe it in detail. The entranced

Reva proceeded to describe the home, the furniture, and even read the manufacturers' labels on various appliances. And then she announced that some people had just arrived and surprised Benzaquin's wife. As she described the new arrivals on the scene, Benzaquin said that her description sounded like friends of theirs from another state whose company neither he nor his wife expected.

During the next commercial, Benzaquin left the set to hurriedly call his wife back in Boston. When he returned, he announced on-air that Reva had been correct. It was, indeed, those friends from another state who had arrived unexpectedly at the Benzaquin home in Boston. And Reva had seen every detail from a comfortable easy chair on a television set in Chicago.

Long-Distance Clairvoyance by a British Seer

During that same period of time, Brad was also conducting experiments in standard clairvoyance with the British psychic John Pendragon. A number of targets were set up, which the mind traveler from Great Britain hit with incredible accuracy. Pendragon also picked up on illnesses, accidents, and other events that occurred in and around Brad's office and home. John Pendragon described his technique for long-distance clairvoyance:

When I am in good psychic form and properly tuned in, I could get impressions while standing on my head. However, I do employ a kind of technique for map reading. I like to have a picture frame about 12"x18" filled with black paper or dull-finished fabric—a sort of "black projection screen," rather like a negativized cinema screen. I find that the screen also helps in receiving clairvoyant impressions other than those connected with my map-dowsing, but it does not put me off not to have it.

I prop the screen up in front of my typewriter if I propose to type as I see the "film." If the machine comes between me and the picture in an obstructive sense, then I just watch the "film." I explore the map with a finger—usually the forefinger of my right hand—and what I am touching on the map usually projects itself on the screen. I find that for best results I must have myself free of emotion and personal worries, calmly poised [and] I must not try. A rather indifferent attitude appears to be best. If I become anxious, the picture either will not come—or if it does, I lose it.

I sometimes use a steel knitting needle as a pointer. A pencil will do, but my forefinger is the best. I like a small-scale map to start with. If, let us say, I should put my finger on a small town in Kansas, I might first see the main street. Then I might take a map of the town itself and run my forefinger up and down the main street, receiving detailed impressions of various buildings, concentrating on various sites. I emphasize that I do not need the screen as a physical crutch in my map-dowsing work. The picture can appear in mid-air. On occasion, there may be no picture at all, but simply a subjective impression.

The Blessed Harmony that Governs the Universe

When the internationally famous psychic-sensitive Olof Jonsson died on May 11, 1998, it was almost as if a member of Brad's family had passed, for the two had participated in countless experiments in the period from 1967 to 1974, and had always remained in touch. Jonsson, perhaps the most powerful physical medium of recent times, was the psychic who participated with astronaut Edgar Mitchell in the Moon to Earth Psi experiment during the Apollo 14 flight.

In Olof Jonsson's view, the human mind/soul is independent of time and space:

> When I am about to try to see something which is not available to my usual senses, I put myself into a half-awake, disconnected state of mind; and I try, mentally, to move very slowly to that place I am about to describe. After a while, when I have found the right mental condition, I see what is presented to me.

> In certain instances, when the conditions are right, I can also move back in time and experience happenings that lead into the past. I can walk on streets in strange cities and observe everyday life as it once existed in the past. I can then move forward and find myself able to account for the many changing environmental scenes.

Olof Jonsson repeatedly emphasized that in order to achieve effective control over Psi phenomena one must first place oneself in a harmonious state of mind. It is this plateau of tranquility, this sense of oneness with the universe, that Olof insisted must be acquired. Spontaneous Psi may occur at any time without any kind of warning. Such phenomena may be subjectively meaningful to the individual, but in order to control these powers as an experienced psychic controls them, one must have a "harmonious state of mind." He goes on to explain:

> This state comes about best when one relaxes and frees oneself from all irritating conditions and concerns. Become, for a moment, a little is- land unto yourself. When you feel the conditions are right, try a little experiment in telepathy. At- tempt to transmit a letter or a number to some- one present in the room. When you achieve a particular point of certainty and sufficient readi- ness, you can try more difficult things, such as the transference of whole statements.

Olof was convinced that all the Psi abilities lay latent in everyone and could be brought out to a high degree in those persons who chose to enter a program of training and development. "As with all meaningful goals in life," he said, "the development of any of the Psi talents demand purposeful practice and belief in one- self."

A truly humble man who harbored no hidden agen- das, Jonsson resisted all opportunities to become a psychic reader, a channel for the other side, or a guru with thousands of disciples. He once said:

> To be able to control these powers, these "sparks of divinity" within each of us, never tempt the wise to make a religion out of spiritual blessings that have been dispensed to all persons. Rather,

an awareness of the powers within should serve
to equip the interested and the receptive with a
brilliant searchlight on the path to Cosmic Harmony.

It is in one's own home, in one's own little chamber, in moments of quiet meditation that a
stream of the great light of the Comos is best able
to reach in and enrich the soul and open the eyes
to the magnificent and tranquil gardens that lie
beyond the borders of the Unexplained. That
which governs a person's life is neither chemistry
nor physics nor anything material, but the proper
spiritual linkup with the powers within one's own
psyche and the blessed Harmony that governs
the Universe.

FOURTEEN

THE GREAT MYSTERY

In our journey through the unexplained, the most important key has remained just beyond our reach, a key that would enable us to open the door to the unknown and obtain a clearer image of the Source behind all phenomena.

That extremely crucial key to understanding the mysteries of the unexplained is *Time*. A.S. Eddington, an early psychical researcher, once observed: "In any attempt to bridge the domains of experience belonging to the spiritual and physical sides of nature, Time occupies the key position."

Even when a clairvoyant, a psychic sensitive, a prophet, or a remote viewer receives an accurate glimpse of a future event, it is perhaps not so much a question of our free will as it is a matter of what constitutes Time.

For more than 2,000 years, clerics, scientists, psychical researchers, and historians have recorded true precognitions. The Bible and other holy books include a remarkable collection of divinely inspired prophecies and promises. Through the centuries of cerebral human existence, a large and impressive argument has been building up which indicates that our mundane human conception of Time as an absolute is an extremely naive one.

H.F. Saltmarsh has theorized that what we call the "present moment" is not a point of Time, but a small time interval called the "specious present." According to his theory, our subconscious minds have a much larger "specious present" than our conscious level of being. For the subconscious, all events would be occurring in the "present." If, on occasion, some of this subconscious knowledge were to burst into the conscious, it would be interpreted as either a memory of a past event or a precognition of a future event.

Each of us knows that our past is neatly catalogued somewhere in our subconscious. Saltmarsh is suggesting that all events—past, present, and future—are part of the "present" for the deeper, transcendent level of our mind.

The Eternal Now

In his *An Experiment with Time*, J.W. Dunne provides examples of his own precognitive dreams recorded over a period of many years. Dunne firmly believes in sleep and dreams as the prime openers of the subconscious. He formulated a philosophy, which he called "Serialism," to account for precognition. In his view, Time was an "Eternal Now." All events that have ever occurred, that exist now, or that ever will be, are everlastingly in existence.

In our ordinary, conscious, waking state, our view is only of the present. In sleep or altered states of consciousness, however, our view might be sufficiently enlarged to permit several glimpses of the future.

Time Exists in a Sphere or Dimension of Its Own

"Time," moaned a puzzled St. Augustine, "what is it? If nobody asks me, I know. But if I am asked, I don't know!"

It is probably apparent to most readers of this book that the conventional view of linear Time existing as some sort of stream flowing along in one dimension is an inadequate one. In this view, the past no longer exists; it is gone forever. The future doesn't exist because it has not yet occurred. The only thing that exists is the present moment.

But wait. The present doesn't really exist, either, since it is no sooner "now" than that "now" becomes a part of the past. What was the future when you began reading this sentence is fleetingly the present and has already become the past by the time you have read the next word.

If the past completely ceased to exist, then we should have no memory of it. Yet each of us has a large and vastly varied memory bank. Therefore, the past must exist in some sense, perhaps not as a physical or material reality, but in some sphere or dimension of its own. Similarly, the future must also exist in some way in a sphere or dimension of its own. And for that transcendent level of our mind, there is no differentiation between past, present, and future. All dimensions of Time exist as aspects of the Eternal Now.

Here is a useful analogy that many have found helpful in gaining a better understanding of the dimensions of Time:

You are riding on the rear platform of a train. You look to the left and to the right. As the train chugs along, you are able to see a panorama of new scenes as they come into your view.

As the train continues, those scenes fade into the distance and are lost to view. They have become your past. But you know that those scenes do not cease to exist after they have passed from your view—and you are also aware that they were in existence before you perceived them, even though you were only able to see them at the time that they were your present.

However, if another person were flying high above the train in an airplane, he or she would be able to see the train's past and present, as well as future scenes lying ahead far beyond your limited ground-level view. All would exist for the person in the airplane as an "Eternal Now."

In the words of philosopher Alfred North Whitehead, "It is impossible to meditate on Time and the mystery of the creative passage of Nature without an overwhelming emotion at the limitations of human intelligence."

Time and Human Imagination

If human intelligence is limited, philosopher and ethnobiologist Terence McKenna commented that the human imagination has no discernible boundaries: "In the imagination, all information throughout space and time is somehow accessible."

In the contemporary philosopher's opinion, the human imagination is capable of receiving transmissions from elsewhere in the universe and it looms as our most reliable location for the living space of the future. McKenna believes that:

> The imagination is the largest part of us, and where we are to spend most of the rest of human history. I think the human imagination is as solid as the real estate you're standing on. When this is understood, there will be a kind of migration into the human imagination. You know, time travel, space flight, immortality.

McKenna, author of such works as *Archaic Revival* and *Food of the Gods*, has foreseen that in 2012, Time will cease to be linear because the technology will be created which will cause Time to lose its linear and serial quality. Such technology is possible, he maintains, because the human mind is not locally bound to Earth.

According to McKenna:

> This is where our mistake has been—to think that we make up what we imagine. We don't. We see what we imagine...Your eyes show you three-dimensional states, and your imagination shows you everything else. And in that everything else there are things we resonate with—races, beings, minds, situations.

Identifying the Source, the Great Mystery

And now we must examine the Great Mystery. If we humans are capable of transcending all physical boundaries with our imagination, could we, in turn, be the products of some Higher Intelligence's imagination?

And would that same Higher Intelligence be the source of the energy that creates all the phenomena that make up the unexplained? Are ghosts, angels, demons, UFOs, alien beings, and a host of other multi-dimensional creatures all products of this single source?

Is this Source extraterrestrial or multidimensional in nature, and has it fashioned a planetary environment of goblins and ghosts as instructional devices to bring our species into a higher awareness of the true nature of the universe?

Could this Source be what all human cultures and traditions have come to label their concept of God? Could it be a supernatural Supreme Creator Being that manifests images of angels and demons to order to shepherd our species, the product of its own divine creative energy, to an eventual unity with its sublime and perfect wholeness?

Or have we, in our frightening evolutionary trek from hairless ape to astronaut, created these deities, monsters, and merry woodland spirits from our own imagination to assuage the desperate loneliness that we have felt staring into the vast and seemingly endless expanse of the night sky?

Are We Only Listening to Our Brain Talking to Itself?

In the early 1980s, Julian Jaynes stated in his *The Origin of Consciousness in the Breakdown of the Bicameral Mind* that the "voice of divinity" that prophets and seers have heard down through the ages is simply the brain talking to itself. According to his thesis, humankind existed for thousands of centuries, functioning ant-like in colonies and being directed by hallucinatory voices that survive today in schizophrenics. These inner voices were assumed by primitive humankind to be divine, and they gave rise to all religions.

Even though humans developed language around 100,000 BCE, according to Jaynes, they had no inner existence (consciousness) until around 10,000 BCE. In those intervening thousands of years, men and women moved about as sleepwalkers, functional, but unaware. Like rats set loose in a maze, they could solve rudimentary problems, but they possessed no abilities of introspection, imagination, or projection to past or future. Without consciousness, early humans were guided primarily by habit.

But new situations were constantly arising in their environment, producing stress and the need for new forms of action, thus necessitating the creation of the inner voices as aids in problem solving. Such interior guidance, the commingled side effects of language and primitive self-assertion, permitted the early humans to remain at survival tasks for longer periods of time.

Eventually, the human brain evolved to integrate the voices. Humans became "bicameral," utilizing the left side of the brain for speech, the right hemisphere for the production of the interior dictator.

And as the brain evolved, so did the society that it produced. By about 1000 BCE, Jaynes theorizes, human culture had grown too complicated to be controlled by the simple commands of the inner voices. Certainly the written word did a great deal to undermine the godlike authority of the voices, although certain of the final pronouncements of the gods, which were written down, may have become the beginning of law, both ecclesiastical and secular.

In Jaynes' view, then, the "voices of the gods" are subdued in contemporary humankind because we are more firmly fixed in a conscious world. The voices of the right side of the brain still do break through, he suggests, as in the cases of such figures as Joan of Arc, contemporary mystics, UFO channelers, drug users, and schizophrenics.

Does Evolution Have Us In Its Ultimate Plan?

During a television appearance in Nashville, Brad set forth his hypothesis that whatever the UFO enigma was, it appeared to have as one of its goals the act of pulling humankind steadily into the future. Before he left the studio, a call came in from a prominent local psychiatrist inviting the author to dinner.

Over dinner that evening, the psychiatrist put forth his theory that evolution itself was responsible for UFOs, the appearance of alien life forms, and most of the other unexplained phenomena. It is evolution itself that creates these anthropomorphic images and utilizes them to keep humankind moving steadily toward the future. That is why UFOs have always appeared to be of a technology just in advance of terrestrial science.

Evolution has a grand plan for humankind, the apex of its creation, and it constantly fashions mental devices to encourage *Homo sapiens* to achieve its ultimate planetary goal, which is to leave Earth and populate other planets in the universe.

Found: A "God-Module" in the Human Brain

In November 1997, a team of neuroscientists from the University of California at San Diego announced their discovery of what they termed a "God module" in the human brain that could be responsible for human-kind's evolutionary instinct to believe in religious concepts.

Dr. Vilayanur Ramachandran, head of the research team, admitted that such conclusions were preliminary, but suggested that the initial results of their work indicate that the phenomena of religious beliefs may be "hard-wired" into the human brain as a Darwinian adaptation to encourage cooperation between individuals.

We Are "Hard-Wired" to Perceive a Spiritual Reality

Matthew Alper believes that humans are innately "hard-wired" to perceive a spiritual reality "...to enable us to deal with our unique and otherwise debilitating awareness of death." This "God Part" of the brain, Alper theorizes, is a "cluster of neurons from which our universal spiritual cognitions, perceptions, behaviors, and sentiments are generated."

In Alper's terrestrial cosmology, God is not a supreme power somewhere "out there" in the universe, but is, in actuality, the "product of inherited perception, the manifestation of a biological evolutionary adaptation, a 'spiritual' cognitive function, which exists exclusively in human brains."

Intervention of a Transcendental Agency?

On the other hand, Sir John Eccles, winner of the Nobel Prize for medicine in 1963, is an evolutionist who has declared that the process of evolution alone cannot explain our awareness of ourselves. As the scientist who demonstrated the transmission of electrical impulses in the brain and who was well acquainted with the workings of humankind's mental machinery, Eccles became increasingly convinced of the intervention of some transcendental agency in the infusion of a Soul into *Homo sapiens.*

Simply stated, he theorizes that the brain and the mind are separate entities that interact, but it is only the brain that is the product of genetic evolution. Sir John explained his thinking in an interview with Sandy Rovner of the *Washington Post* (April 1981):

> I am an evolutionist, of course, but I don't believe that evolution is the final story.... The genetic code and natural selection explain quite a lot, but evolution doesn't explain...the evolution of consciousness.... If my uniqueness of self is tied to the genetic uniqueness of self that built my brain, the odds against myself existing are ten to the ten-thousandth against.

> It is just too improbable to wait around to get the right constructed brain for you. The brain is a computer, you see. Each of us has a computer, and we are the programmers of this computer. [We were] born...with what this wonderful structure of evolution and genetic coding have wrought... But the soul is this unique creation that is ours for life. We are experiencing, remembering, creating, suffering, imagining. All of this is processed here with the soul central to it.

A Skeptic Concedes Existence of Ultimate Mysteries

In *Skeptic* magazine (Vol. 5 No. 2 1997), Editor-in-Chief Michael Shermer interviewed Martin Gardner, the prolific science writer, author of *Fads and Fallacies in the Name of Science*, and the founder of the modern skeptical movement. Shermer seemed as surprised as we were when Gardner said that he believed in God, that he sometimes prayed and worshipped, and that he hoped for life after death.

"I call myself a philosophical theist, or sometimes a fideist, who believes something on the basis of emotional reasons rather than intellectual reasons," Gardner explained.

When Shermer pointed out what seemed to be a paradox for a man "so skeptical about so many things," Gardner refers to the classic essay in defense of fideism, William James' *The Will to Believe*:

James' argument, in essence, is that if you have strong emotional reasons for a metaphysical belief, and it is not strongly contradicted by science or logical reasons, then you have a right to make a leap of faith if it provides sufficient satisfaction.

Gardner also identified himself as a "mysterian," explaining that:

There are certain things I regard as ultimate mysteries. Free will is one of those. Another is time. I don't think we have the slightest idea what time is...The same thing is true with space. Time and space are ultimate mysteries. Free will is bound up in the mysteries of time about which we can never understand, at least at this stage of our evolutionary history.

Scientists Can Have Religious Feelings

In his recent book, *Consilience: Unity of Knowledge*, Edward O. Wilson, highly respected biologist and firm advocate of the scientific method, said that as he embarked on his quest for knowledge, he had no desire to purge himself of religious feelings. He was aware that they were bred in him, that they nourished the wellsprings of his creative life:

> I also retained a small measure of common sense. To wit, people must belong to a tribe; they yearn to have a purpose larger than themselves. We are obliged by the deepest drives of the human spirit to make ourselves more than animated dust, and we must have a story to tell about where we came from and why we are here. Could Holy Writ be just the first literate attempt to explain the universe and make ourselves significant within it? Perhaps science is a continuation on new and better-tested ground to attain the same end. If so, then in that sense, science is religion liberated.

An Alive and Conscious Universe

Dr. Edgar Mitchell has often described his visionary experience while on the Moon during Apollo 14 in which he had an overwhelming sense that the universe itself is alive and that it is in some way a conscious being in its own right.

"This means that all life forms, whether on Earth or elsewhere, are all part of one giant consciousness," Mitchell said.

We Are Being Shaped by Something

Terence McKenna envisioned the universe involved in a process of self-metamorphosis:

> I think we are being shaped by something—and some people think it is God Almighty. I'm not willing to go that far. But something is pulling us toward itself in the future. And as we move toward it, in order to be able to understand and tolerate its presence, we are becoming more like it.
>
> So there is a kind of self-transformative process working on us as we move through history toward it. And it represents somehow the completion of this process of transformation. It is the transcendental object.

Humankind Enters an Accelerated Program of Transformation

We are definitely being shaped by "something" outside of ourselves, as opposed to voices or impulses from within our psyches. This energy, force, or intelligence seems dedicated toward pulling our species into the future and accomplishing a process of transformation for all of humankind.

Although this paraphysical, multidimensional intelligence has always been with us, it would seem that the planetary program has been accelerated to accommodate the fast-approaching time of transition and transcendence. Our prophets and revelators have warned us for generations that this period—the Great Cleansing, Armageddon, the Earth Changes—will be a difficult one. We have also been promised that after a season of cataclysmic changes during which an old world dies, a new and better world will be born.

Throughout history, this intelligence, this "Other," has communicated to humankind through the archetypes within the collective human unconscious, appearing in whatever form would be best received by the individual recipient. Within the individual contemporary mystical experience, what may appear to one recipient as an angel may manifest as an extraterrestrial to another.

We are by no means denying the possibility of extraterrestrial visitors. However, we feel that the overwhelming majority of the phenomena that we have encountered during our journey through the unexplained has been manifested by an intelligence that seeks to remind us that all life is one and to bring us back into a sense of wholeness with the Cosmos. Humankind must become truly integrated with the planetary environment, and at the same time, it must learn to make the universe its home.

Whether this intelligence manifests itself as traditional angels, time travelers from the future, advanced human adepts, or crew members of extraterrestrial starships, the very presence of these beings conveys to the human observer that humankind is part of a much larger community of sentient beings. There exists a more complex hierarchy of powers and principalities, a richer kingdom of interrelated species—both physical and nonphysical—than could be imagined by the practitioners and promulgators of conventional thought and beliefs. In addition, the very presence of these entities demonstrates that mechanistic science has been completely transcended and humankind must prepare to cope with an avalanche of new concepts, new thinking, new technology, and new approaches to the Cosmos.

The time of transcendence offers humankind the opportunity for change and the chance to be born again to new and higher dimensions. As we extend our vision to the future, we will see more acutely the need to spiritualize, transcend, transform, and regenerate our body, mind, and spirit.

Certainly one of the central missions of this intelligence has been to teach us how we can become perfected humans, higher-minded beings. We are being conditioned in the practice of elevating our thoughts and emotions to better love our human brothers and sisters, our fellow life forms on the planet, and the Blessed Harmony, the "Source of All That Is" that governs the universe.

BOOKS FOR YOUR OWN
JOURNEY THROUGH THE UNEXPLAINED

Beckley, Timothy Green. *The UFO Silencers.* New Brunswick, NJ: Inner Light, 1990.

Bell, Art. *The Art of Talk.* New Orleans: Paper Chase Press, 1995.
_____. *The Quickening.* New Orleans: Paper Chase Press, 1997.

Braden, Gregg. *Awakening to Zero Point.* Radio Bookstore Press, 1997.

Bramley, William. *The Gods of Eden.* New York: Avon, 1993.

Brinkley, Dannion. *Saved by the Light.* New York: Harper, 1995.

Bryant, Alice and Linda Seeback. *Healing Shattered Reality—Understanding Contactee Trauma.* Tigard, OR: Wild Flower Press, 1991.

Childress, David Hatcher. *Extraterrestrial Archaeology.* Adventures Unlimited Press, 1994.

Clark, Jerome and Loren Coleman. *The Unidentified.* New York: Warner Paperback Library, 1975.

Corso, Col. Philip J. with William J. Birnes. *The Day After Roswell.* New York: Pocket Books, 1997.

Downing, Barry H. *The Bible and Flying Saucers.* New York: Avon, 1970.

Garfield, Patricia. *Creative Dreaming.* New York: Fireside Books, 1995.

Goldberg, Bruce. *Time Travelers from Our Future: An Explanation for Alien Abductions.* St. Paul, MN: Llewellyn Publications, 1998.

Hancock, Graham and Robert Bauval. *The Message of the Sphinx: A Quest for the Hidden Legacy of Mankind.* New York: Crown Books, 1997.

Hoagland, Richard C. *The Monuments of Mars.* North Atlantic Books, 1996.

Hopkins, Budd. *Witnessed—The True Story of the Brooklyn Bridge UFO Abductions.* Pocket Books: New York, 1996.

Howe, Linda Moulton. *Glimpses of Other Realities, Volume 2: High Strangeness.* New Orleans: Paper Chase Press, 1998.

Keel, John A. *The Mothman Prophecies.* New York: Saturday Review Press, 1975.

La Berge, Stephen. *Exploring the World of Lucid Dreaming.* New York: Ballantine, 1991.

McKenna, Terrence. *Archaic Revival.* San Francisco: Harper San Francisco, 1992.

O'Leary, Brian. *Miracle in the Void.* Kamapu's Press, 1996.

Pye, Lloyd. *Everything You Know Is Wrong: Book One—Human Origins.* Adamu Press, 1997.

Randle, Kevin D. *The Randle Report: UFOs in the '90s.* New York: M. Evans, 1997.
_____ and Donald Schmitt. *The Truth About the UFO Crash at Roswell.* New York: M. Evans, 1994.

Sitchin, Zecharia. *The 12th Planet.* New York: Avon, 1978.

Steiger, Brad. *Mysteries of Time and Space.* Englewood Cliffs, NJ: Prentice Hall, 1974. Schiffer Publishing, 1989.
_____ (ed.) *Project Bluebook.* New York: Confucian Press/Ballantine, 1976.
_____ and Hayden Hewes. *Inside Heaven's Gate.* New York: Signet, 1997.

_____ and Edgar R. Fouche. *Alien Rapture: The Chosen.* Lakeville, MN: Galde Press, 1998.

_____ and Sherry Hansen Steiger. *The Rainbow Conspiracy.* New York: Kensington, 1994, 1998.

Strieber, Whitley. *Communion.* New York: Beech Tree/William Morrow, 1987.

_____. *Confirmation: Hard Evidence of Aliens Among Us.* New York: St. Martin's Press, 1998.

Watkins, Leslie. *Alternative 3.* London: Sphere, 1978.

Wolf, Michael. *The Catchers of Heaven: A Trilogy.* Pittsburgh: Dorrance, 1996.

INDEX

Other books from Paper Chase Press

The Art of Talk
Art Bell
hardcover, 240 pages
The Art of Talk is Art Bell's first book. For the first time,
America can learn about the man behind the microphone.
The Art of Talk reveals a life which is as diverse and interesting
as his radio programs.

$24.95

The Quickening: Today's Trends, Tomorrow's World
Art Bell
paperback, 336 pages

The Quickening calls attention to the acceleration of every
aspect of human existence as we head toward the 21st century.
Art Bell astutely examines the underlying forces of today's
trends and offers thoughts on coming to terms with these trends.

$15.95

Glimpses of Other Realities, Vol. 2 High Strangeness
Linda Moulton Howe
paperback, 200 illus. and photos, 512 pages

Weekly commentator on Art Bell's show, "Dreamland," Linda
Moulton Howe is internationally known for her investigations
of crop circles, mysterious animal mutilations, human abduction
syndrome, and apparent extraterrestrial beings interacting with
earth.

$19.95

Other books from Paper Chase Press

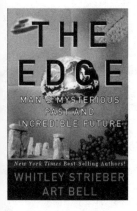

The Edge: Man's Mysterious Past & Incredible Future
Whitley Strieber and Art Bell
hardcover, 272 pages

Bestselling authors Whitley Strieber and Art Bell collaborate in this compelling explanation of the great mysteries of past civilizations and how we can use these ancient secrets to overcome the world's greatest challenges.

$24.95

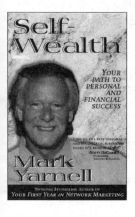

Self Wealth: Your Path to Personal & Financial Success
Mark Yarnell
hardcover, 240 pages

"*Self-Wealth* is one of the best personal and financial achievement books I've read in years!"
-Scott DeGarmo, Publisher,
Success Magazine

$21.95

Other books from Paper Chase Press

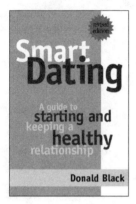

Smart Dating: Starting and Keeping a Healthy Relationsh
Donald Black
paperback, 256 pages

Donald Black, bestselling author and creator of the successful *Smart Dating* workshops, has guided thousands through the sometimes challenging world of dating and relationships.

"Black doesn't believe games, tricks, or formulas lead to perfect relationships... He gives you the principles that work and point in the right direction."
Tucson Citizen

"*Smart Dating* is a book every single person should keep on their night stand."
The Norman Transcript

"*Smart Dating* is straightforward and easy-to-read... definitely will work to your advantage."
Hugh B. Jones, President, Southeast Singles Assoc.
$14.95

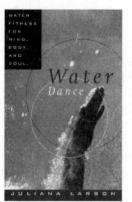

Water Dance: Water Fitness for Mind, Body and Soul
Juliana Larson
paperback, 240 pages

Juliana Larson presents true stories and inspirational guidance for women nurturing women as they experience the fun, freedom, spiritual and physical rewards of sharing while working out in water.
$14.95

To order or to ask for a FREE
Paper Chase Press catalog,

call 1-800-864-7991, or fill out the form:

Please send me _____ copy(ies) of *The Art of Talk*, hardcover

Please send me _____ copy(ies) of *The Quickening*, paperback

Please send me _____ copy(ies) of *Glimpses of Other Realities, Vol.2*, paperback

Please send me _____ copy(ies) of *The Edge*, hardcover

Please send me _____ copy(ies) of *Self Wealth*, hardcover

Please send me _____ copy(ies) of *Smart Dating*, paperback

Please send me _____ copy(ies) of *Water Dance*, paperback

Name _____

Address _____

_____

_____

_____

Signature (for credit card purchases) _____

Please indicate credit card: Visa _____ MC _____ _____

Credit card number _____ **expires** _____

Fill out form and send a check or money order in US funds only.

All payments made to: PAPER CHASE PRESS.

Send to: Paper Chase Press, 5721 Magazine St., Suite 152, New Orleans LA 70115

Add $5.00 S&H for each book ordered in the US (call for outside of US).

Allow up to 4 weeks for delivery.